Praise for *Prioritize!*

This book is a treasure! It is loaded with practical and insightful strategies to catapult your business and your life into extraordinary dimensions. Read it. Study it. Live it. It'll influence your beliefs, enhance your behaviors, and increase your results!

Nido Qubein
Chairman, Great Harvest Bread Company
Founder, National Speakers Association Foundation

Prioritize! **is a great review of the basics and has some very enlightening new ideas that would help virtually anyone putting a high priority on leading their business and their life!**

Barnett Helzberg, Jr.
Author of *What I Learned Before I Sold to Warren Buffett*

Not a better strategic planning resource on the market today! ***Prioritize!*** **gives you the tools to develop and implement a successful business plan that works. New thinking and doing is what makes** ***Prioritize!*** **a winner!**

Robert A. Shively, CAE
CEO, National Auctioneers Association

These words will renew your sense of purpose and re-ignite your passion for making a difference in your world, personally and professionally.

Glenna Salsbury, CSP
CPAE Speaker Hall of Fame

Crisp, clear, concise, and compelling, this book guides you through the steps you can take in achieving significant business success.

Eric Allenbaugh, Ph. D.
Author of *Deliberate Success*

As a long-time user of the *Prioritize!* System, I know that it is the simplest way to execute your company's strategic plan. I've worked with Joe and Bruce for over 15 years and consider them to be men of great integrity. Their wisdom is timeless.

Minaz Abji
Executive Vice President, Host Marriott Corporation

Each time Joe or Bruce speaks or writes, it is with deep thought and conviction. *Prioritize!* is a reflection of their beliefs. I highly recommend the book not only because it is articulated so beautifully and clearly but more so because of the integrity of the authors.

A.C. "Acey" Lampe, Ph.D.
Marketing Division, Hallmark Cards

This is whole life planning made simple. It's an old cliché, but too many people fail to plan, and thereby plan to fail. This book will help you get on with your life.

Ron Willingham
CEO, Integrity Systems, Author of *Integrity Selling for the 21st Century*

Joe Calhoon has long been driven by helping others become successful. His experience and study have resulted in a deceptively simple and exceedingly practical 'How To' approach to building a successful organization.

Lloyd Hill
Chairman, Applebee's International

It is creative, clever, easy to read, and full of useful wisdom. By remembering what our priorities are, the business aspect just naturally falls into place.

Vicki L. Freed, CTC
Senior Vice President of Sales and Marketing, Carnival Cruise Lines

Succeeding in business is a lot like winning in the NFL. You develop a game plan, execute the plan, and adapt as the game goes on. *Prioritize!* helps businesses and people do just that. I highly recommend it!

Len Dawson
Hall of Fame Quarterback, 1970 Superbowl MVP

Our company has been working with Joe for the past five years, so when I recommend you embrace *Prioritize!* it is not a suggestion, it is a testimonial! Earnings are increasing, our people are more productive, and we are having FUN doing it!

Kent Shoemaker
Executive Vice President, FreshPoint, Inc.

This book will help you focus on what's really important to your business and develop the plan required to make it a success!

Tom Hopkins
Author of *How to Master the Art of Selling*

***Prioritize!*...more than a book about planning, more than a book about mission and strategy...this is a book you must read and implement to lead your business and your life on purpose—powerfully!**

Naomi Rhode, CSP
CPAE Speaker Hall of Fame

***Prioritize!* is helping us sell and serve more customers and create greater prosperity for our associates. This is an enlightened approach to business that promotes character, competence, and contribution. I highly recommend it!**

Randy Reed
President, Randy Reed Automotive Group

Joe and Bruce have captured and simplified the elements of leading a business and life successfully. I plan to re-read *Prioritize!* several times and apply its principles to my own business and life. Thank you, Joe and Bruce, for your insight and your ability to make something difficult so approachable and achievable.

Ed Callaghan
Author of *Sell On Purpose, Not By Accident*

***Prioritize!* has been a tremendous plus for Copiah Bank. We now have a clear and concise plan, and priority setting and regular review keeps us on track to achieve our goals.**

George R. Marx
President and CEO, Copiah Bank, N.A.

Working with the *Prioritize!* process for the past year has us pulling together like never before. We're on the same page as we build a solid platform for future growth. *Prioritize!* has produced outstanding results for our organization.

Mike Stange
Vice President and General Manager, Sandestin Golf & Beach Resort

The *Prioritize!* System has changed the way we approach our business. As a result, employee ownership, teamwork, and goal achievement have all dramatically improved. We're getting more done in less time, making more money, and having more fun doing it!

Dan Bashaw
President, Overland Tool, Inc.

***Prioritize!* taps into years and years of leadership wisdom. It allows the reader to skip the fads and distractions found in so many books on business advice.**

Hans Helmerich
President, Helmerich & Payne

PRIORITIZE!

A System for Leading Your Business and Life on Purpose

by Joe Calhoon and Bruce Jeffrey

INSIGHT PUBLISHING
SEVIERVILLE, TENNESSEE

Prioritize!

A System for Leading Your Business and Life on Purpose

By Joe Calhoon and Bruce Jeffrey

Published by Insight Publishing Company
P.O. Box 4189
Sevierville, Tennessee 37864

Printed in Canada

10 9 8 7 6 5 4 3 2

ISBN: 1-932863-28-1

Dedication

This book is dedicated to all the business people who have paved the way by developing products and services, delivering value to customers, and creating jobs for those hard-working souls who put it all together.

This book is also dedicated to all those who have yet to find their way into the wonderful world of enterprise. It is our hope that all readers will find a brighter path and more prosperous future for themselves and their loved ones.

And lastly, this book is dedicated to all who have taught us and continue to teach us these lessons in leadership. As Peter Drucker is fond of saying, "The reason we call it a consulting practice is because we're all still practicing."

Thank you all for the contributions and inspiration you provide.

Table of Contents

"The purpose of life is a life of purpose."

~Robert Byrne

Foreword

by Bob Buford

You will get a lot out of this book. Why? Because planning works. Planning provides the means to transform a river of good intentions into results, performance, and a satisfied life. Planning converts latent energy to active energy. Planning channels passion. Planning gives the focus that evolves a puddle of possibility into a shooting stream of power and intensity.

The second reason you will greatly benefit from this book is that the two men who have assembled this approach have provided the helpful framework to empower *your* energy. For 40 years (20 years each), they have gone to school with the masters of the art of planning. They have invested hours, days, and years of face-to-face work applying these practices to help real people in real situations turn wishes, dreams and frustrations into successful businesses and more fulfilled lives.

You're not just gleaning from one person's wisdom and experience in *Prioritize!* Joe Calhoon and Bruce Jeffrey have distilled the insights and thought-provoking questions of the best teachers and practitioners from diverse backgrounds. For you, planning is demystified. The cookies are on the lowest shelf. I'm not speculating—I have seen this work for people firsthand.

Oliver Wendell Holmes has famously touted "the simplicity on the other side of complexity." Well, these guys can help you develop "a plan on a page" and then make it happen. Most of us suffer not from a lack of options about how to proceed but from the opposite problem. We are like St. James' "double minded man…unstable in all his ways." There are too many options. Which path do we choose? Following the time and experience-tested processes that Calhoon and Jeffrey have made so accessible in these pages can lead you to resolution, action, and results in your business. And, perhaps even more than that, in the final section of the book there's help for clarifying one's sense of calling. Peter Drucker, the most seminal of all the management thinkers, has told me, "We no longer have an economic problem. We have an existential problem." Most of us face the problems of abundance, not the problems of scarcity. Thankfully, in this book there's also help on the way for those problems, more personal in nature. And it comes from men who have not only good processes, but good hearts.

So proceed with enthusiasm. You are in good hands here.[1]

---

[1] Bob Buford has written four books including the best seller, *Halftime*. His most recent book is *Finishing Well*, based on inspiring interviews with sixty remarkable people who are achieving significance in Life II. He led Buford Television, Inc. for 28 years, founded Leadership Network and was Founding Chairman of The Peter F. Drucker Foundation for Nonprofit Management.

Introduction

It doesn't have to be this hard, does it?

We have worked with hundreds of businesses over the past two decades, and we've observed that often in business, we're our own worst enemy. Clients don't get served well, we keep the wrong people too long, and we underperform financially. We're so busy putting out the fires we've created that we don't take the time to do some fire prevention. The result? The fires keeping multiplying.

> *Looking back, my life seems to be one long obstacle course, with me as the chief obstacle.*
>
> *– JACK PARR*

If you think there may be a simpler, smarter, easier way to lead your business, this book is for you.

Who should read this book?

We wrote this book for you, the hard-working people who own, operate, or lead businesses. While our system has also been found to be effective in the non-profit arena and the public sector, the language and examples are primarily from the world of business. Here are some people that have benefited from our approach:

- Business Owners
- Board Members
- Executives
- Department Heads
- Managers
- Team Leaders

Why should you read this book?

We've seen business leaders struggle with five main issues:

1. Leadership Fundamentals
2. Keeping everyone on the same page
3. Making consistent progress
4. Adjusting easily to change
5. Living on purpose

Without always being able to say it, what they're missing is a leadership *system*, a coherent set of tools and practices that would enable their business and their lives to consistently move forward in positive ways. Instead of creating a system that insures regular progress, they do what they've seen other business leaders do—solve problems and hold meetings. Sometimes in despair, they cancel the meetings because they realize the problems are not getting solved.

The number of entrepreneurs—men and women, young and old—who are launching and building companies today is unprecedented. Large companies are trying to become more like smaller, entrepreneurial firms. New growth enterprises are the engine of job and wealth creation.

—RAY SMILOR

To counter this downward spiral, we went to work to create a leadership system for effectively leading a business. We compared notes on the hundreds of clients we have worked with, studied hundreds of articles and books by the best thinkers, and gleaned the best lessons from our own experience.

We knew that the system had to be simple and easy to use. It needed to be cost effective, it had to produce results, and we wanted to give our clients a competitive advantage in their marketplace.

And so *Prioritize!* was born.

A few clients were willing to give it a try, in part because they knew us and liked working with us in the past, and in part because what we were saying was making a little bit of sense to them. We learned a lot from these early clients, and we began to adjust our approach to better meet their needs.

The system we present to you in this book is the result of several years' cultivating, watering, and weeding. It will keep growing and changing because our clients keep improving it, but we felt it was time to release it to a wider audience.

What kind of results can you expect?

Recently we contracted with a consulting firm to analyze the results our clients are experiencing from *Prioritize!* Here are some of the benefits our clients say they are receiving from this approach:

- ✓ Focus and hope
- ✓ An objective view of their company
- ✓ A real-time tool to manage every aspect of their business
- ✓ A manageable and fun life
- ✓ Better communication and cooperation
- ✓ Overall buy-in from the entire staff
- ✓ A stronger management team
- ✓ Measurable goals achieved
- ✓ Higher levels of commitment
- ✓ A competitive advantage

If you're interested in seeing these results in your company, read on.

How We've Organized Our Approach

Let us introduce you to this simple approach to leading your business and life.

The first section, "Lead," explores the demand for leaders to understand and apply the leadership fundamentals that underlie business success.

The next three sections explore the practical application of *Prioritize!* "The First Practice: Clarify" shows you how to develop a dynamic One Page Strategic Plan that includes the six elements for getting everyone on the same page. "The Second Practice: Execute" reveals the essential habits for making progress. And "The Third Practice: Renew" shows you how to adjust your course and keep everyone with you.

We walk you through an example of how to use Clarify, Execute, and Renew in "Apply." You'll see how easy it is to implement these practices to advance your own business and create a high-performing organization.

They know enough who know how to learn.
– *HENRY ADAMS*

And because good organizations are made up of good people, "Live," helps individuals find their calling, make their unique contribution and expand their capacity in order to lead a deeply fulfilling life.

We applaud you for your desire in wanting to improve your business and to achieve higher performance in a way that's sane and straightforward. We'd love to hear from you on how your journey is going. Please send us your story at ourjourney@prioritize.com

And now for the heart of the matter. Growing your business and life is just about to get a whole lot simpler.

Joe Calhoon & Bruce Jeffrey
Kansas City, MO

PART 1

LEAD

A Call to Lead

This book is a call to lead—in our organizations and our lives. To narrow the gap between the way our organizations are performing and the way we'd like our organizations to be performing. To narrow the gap between the way we're living our lives and the way we'd like to be living our lives. It's about working effectively with others to seize opportunities and fulfill dreams.

The world has a desperate need for leadership that can translate vision into reality. Organizations languish, businesses suffer, families struggle. The world community is in turmoil, and the stakes are getting higher. The ability of a few people to do great harm threatens our livelihoods and our communities.

The absence or ineffectiveness of leadership implies the absence of vision, a dreamless society, and this will result, at best, in the maintenance of the status quo or, at worst, in the disintegration of our society because of lack of purpose and cohesion.

—WARREN BENNIS & BURT NANUS

While the need for leadership is acute in all sectors of society, the need for strong, effective, moral leadership in the business world is especially keen.

Business provides value—for customers, employees, owners, and the larger community. This value provides the foundation on which all other segments of society are built. The taxes that businesses pay on their profits and that employees pay on their earnings fund government programs. Individuals use the wages and dividends they get from business to support non-profit organizations, places of worship, and schools. Without the extra value created by businesses, the impact of these vital institutions would be diminished.

It's easy to see that if businesses don't succeed, then our whole society can disintegrate rapidly. American enterprise has created the most prosperous nation in the history of the world, but the past doesn't guarantee the future. Much depends on the people willing to take the risks and invest their resources to create businesses that bless many.

Leading a business is not a task for the faint-hearted. We know. We've been there—both with our own businesses and with other owners, managers, partners, and team members. It's challenging and it's thrilling. It's exasperating and deeply fulfilling, and we love it.

Leaders acknowledge the reality they live in. They envision a better future. They work to make that better future a reality.

Leaders know that *significance emerges when vision is coupled with execution—vision shapes the future and execution fulfills the dream.*

The world needs your leadership, your vision, and your ability to bring vision into being. It needs it now more than ever.

Three Growing Leadership Challenges

The question is, what are the demands on leadership today? We think there are three growing challenges to leading effectively:

- Life and business are getting more complex
- We hesitate in the face of so many choices
- One person is not sufficient to lead an organization

Complexity

The environment in which we live is creating enormous complexity, making leadership difficult. There's more information to deal with and more demands on our time. Our customers want more, our employees expect more, and profit performance is essential.

We want more. We want to have good families, great relationships, and healthier lives. We want financial prosperity and security. We want to make a difference.

We're living in a smaller, more complex world than ever before. Technology tries to help, but can sometimes exacerbate this complexity. Ever-present mobile phones, mobile computers, voice mail and email demand that we be more responsive than ever before.

In all of this complexity, how does one lead?

Hesitancy

The number of choices we face every day can be daunting. Even going to the store to buy bread isn't easy! Standing there looking at all the options can be an adventure in itself.

Even more so with our choices about where to live, what to buy, what world view to adopt. We have more choices than at any time in history about what to read, how to enjoy free time, and with whom to associate. We have choices about what to watch on TV, what to listen to on the radio (or the CD player, the mini-disk player, the MP3 player, or the Ipod). We can choose from a bigger variety of foods and restaurants, of diet plans and fitness routines.

Choices take time and thought. How can we lead without being paralyzed by the overwhelming number of choices we have to make?

One is Not Enough

The myth of the omni-competent leader is crumbling. As Warren Bennis and co-author David Hennan point out in *Co-Leaders* and Jim Collins in *Good to Great,* leadership is much more than a charismatic hero. High-performing organizations require leadership teams, and they require leaders at all levels.

New questions are arising: how does one assemble a team of leaders? When filling a vacancy, what competencies are necessary in the new person that will complement the talents and abilities of the people already in place? How do you work a plan that engages the entire team's commitment?

Simple, Clear, Together

What emerges from these challenges is the new dimension of leadership, which we explore in this book—the new call for effectiveness at all levels in organizations. The demand for leaders today is to keep things *simple, clear,* and *together.*

Simple. Clear. Together.

The *Prioritize!* system of leadership will help you develop the basic skills for leading effectively. You will learn how to simplify your organizational demands to a few key priorities. You will execute those priorities better than ever before. And you will quickly adapt to change and keep your whole team on board and engaged.

We discovered the *Prioritize!* system as we observed hundreds of companies and thousands of leaders and gleaned from them habits of thinking and doing that made them effective. We'd like to start by sharing one of our favorite corporate success stories.

Mr. K – Billions Built On Three Principles

Joe: In the mid 1980's I had the privilege of interviewing a man recognized as one of our nation's most successful entrepreneurs. Ewing Kauffman, lovingly called "Mr. K" by his associates, started a business in the basement of his home in 1950 with $5,000 and a few decades later was leading one of America's great companies. At the time of our meeting, Mr. K was a billionaire and more than 300 Marion Labs associates had become millionaires working with his company. In a document I received that day, Marion's purpose was clearly stated: "Helping others is the cornerstone upon which the success and reputation of Marion Laboratories, Inc. has been built. For more than three decades, the Kansas City-

All the money in the world cannot solve problems unless we work together. And, if we work together, there is no problem in the world that can stop us.

– EWING MARION KAUFFMAN

based pharmaceutical company has dedicated its resources, research, and marketing efforts to providing products that help people to lead healthy and productive lives."

When I asked Mr. K how they had built such a high-performing organization (with more sales per associate than any company in their industry) he said they built the business on three fundamental principles.

Principle #1

Those who produce should share in the results. He said, "This principle came about because I worked for another pharmaceutical company on straight commission. No salary, no car, just commission and I just fell in love with the business. The second year I made more money than the president, which was a mistake. So, they cut my commission. By this time, I had six sales people working for me. I stayed another year, did the same thing and they cut my territory. So, I quit and started Marion in the basement of my home on $5,000." Mr. K went on to tell me that he thought that the two biggest mistakes that business people make are that they don't give their people a share of the profits and they don't give their people enough authority.

> *It used to be that the head of the organization was the intellectual one who made all the decisions. That's not true anymore. Today you will find that at all levels there is ability you should be drawing on.*
>
> *– EWING MARION KAUFFMAN*

Because Marion associates contributed so effectively to the enterprise, they received 15% annual profit sharing; they also received a one-week, two-week, or four-week annual bonus based on their job performance. In the previous year alone, people who gave useful suggestions had received $400,000.

Principle #2

Treat others the way you would like to be treated. Mr. K explained to me that at Marion, if you talked about someone behind their back, the first time you were warned, the second time you were fired. He said it was a tough rule to live with, but it was great for morale. Everyone knew that if someone had a problem with them they would display the courage and consideration to confront them directly. He felt it was a key to creating and sustaining a high-performing organization. He went on to say, "Treating other people the way you want to be treated is the finest way to make money that there is... It's the most intelligent principle of business that there is...and you're happier. That's the nicest thing. You make more money, and you're happier."

When you have a problem with a person, focus on the problem, not the personality.

– EWING MARION KAUFFMAN

Principle #3

Give back to the community. The Kauffman Foundation, a billion dollar philanthropy he founded, is now a reflection of Mr. K's third principle. Its purpose is to stimulate the development of youth and the free enterprise system. Thousands of lives are being impacted as a result of Mr. K's philanthropy.

Mr. K was an exemplary leader, and he understood the role of leadership. He once said, "You don't *manage* people. I don't want to be *managed,* but I don't mind being *led.*"

Personal Success Stories

Many thousands of individuals are leading their businesses and lives on purpose. Consider track coach Bill Bowerman. One morning in 1971, Bill's wife was making waffles for breakfast, when it suddenly occurred to him to place rubber in the waffle iron to make better running shoes. Bill is the co-founder of Nike. Today the Waffle Sole is used in virtually every running and hiking shoe.

If we all did the things we are capable of doing, we would literally astound ourselves.

– THOMAS EDISON

Thomas Edison set up a laboratory in his basement at age 10, Bill Gates wrote his first computer program at 13, Henry Ford quit school to become an engineer at 16.

Age, gender, geography, education, and race seem to make little difference as related to the contributions people make in their business and personal lives.

Actress Brooke Shields starred in her first commercial before her first birthday and world-renowned investor Warren Buffet earned money selling Coca-Cola to friends at the age of 6. Ray Kroc didn't start McDonalds until he was 52, and Colonel Sanders founded Kentucky Fried Chicken when he was 65.

While Mozart gave keyboard concerts across Europe at 6, and Julie Andrews mastered a four-octave singing range at 8, jazz pianist Eubie Blake didn't start his recording company until he was 89. Consider these other examples of business and personal achievement:

> *We cannot become what we need to be by remaining what we are.*
>
> *–MAX DePREE*

- Natalie Wood starred in *Miracle on 34th Street* at 9
- Bill Gates co-founded Microsoft at 19
- Berry Gordy started Motown Records at 29
- Janet Guthrie became the first woman to drive in the Indy 500 at 39
- Julia Child first experienced culinary fame at 49
- Satchel Paige pitched for the Kansas City A's at 59
- Noah Webster published his American Dictionary of the English Language at 69
- Ben Franklin invented bifocals at 79
- Frank Lloyd Wright completed his work on the Guggenheim Museum at 89
- Otto Bucher scored a hole-in-one at 99

And at age 77, Ben Franklin helped America win recognition of its independence, Mahatma Gandhi quieted religious violence in India, and astronaut John Glenn traveled in space.

These examples and hundreds more are captured in Andrew Postman's wonderful little book, *There's Always Time for Greatness.*

So, what are you capable of achieving? Far more than you think and it's never too early or too late to start. It is our hope that this book will help you achieve extraordinary results in your life and your business.

Thinking, Behavior, and Results

A useful definition of insanity is to keep doing the same thing over and over and expect different results. Common sense dictates that to change our results, we need to change our behavior.

So how do we change our behavior? We must change our thinking. Stephen R. Covey calls it a "paradigm shift." Others call it changing your attitude, changing your philosophy or getting your head straight.

Good thinking creates good behavior, which creates good results. In the same manner, bad thinking creates bad behavior, which creates bad results.

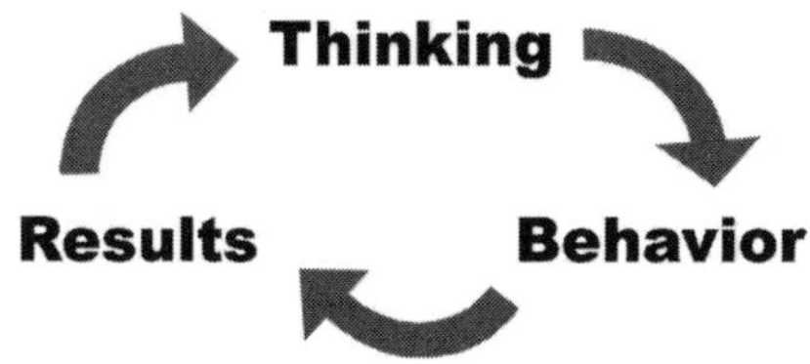

Let's explore some sound ways of thinking and behaving on these six fundamentals so we can get better results.

1. Give, then Receive
2. Working with People
3. Visionary Leaders and Operational Leaders
4. The Purpose of a Business
5. The Wisdom of 80/20
6. Clarify and Simplify

Leadership Fundamental #1: Give, Then Receive

Joe: In 1983, I made a decision to become a full-time speaker, trainer, and business consultant. My first mentor was Cavett Robert.

Each year the National Speakers Association gives an award called "The Cavett." It's like an Emmy or an Oscar for professional speakers, but it's not based solely on performance. The primary criterion for receiving the award is *giving*. The Cavett Award is a tribute to the spirit of Cavett Robert. Cavett was one of the most giving, caring, loving people I've ever known.

> *Give and it shall be given unto you.*
>
> *– SAINT LUKE*

So it won't surprise you that as I began my career, Cavett advised me, "If it's worth doing for fee, it's worth doing for free until people will pay you for it." So, I spoke for free.

Anywhere.

Everywhere.

Any place they'd have me, I'd deliver my message: Rotary, Kiwanis, Lions, and Chambers of Commerce. Years later, I could trace back virtually every piece of business to someone who had heard me give one of those free speeches.

There you have it—give, and you receive.

The most prosperous people we know—the ones who are overflowing in health, happiness, friends, strong families, as well as financially, are the ones who are consistently giving. They give their time, their talent, and their insights. They give encouragement, service, advice, and new ideas. They give and give and give, and their lives, as well as their businesses, overflow with prosperity.

Give and you'll receive.

It's the fundamental natural law that creates all true business and personal success. The power of giving goes beyond our human comprehension.

A man there was, and they called him mad; the more he gave, the more he had.

–JOHN BUNYAN

In business, your company provides goods and services valued by your customers. It supplies work, compensation, and benefits valued by team members. It returns profit to the owners. Your business gives and these individuals give back—time, talent, and investment.

In life, you provide leadership, love, encouragement, and kindness to your loved ones. You provide service to your place of worship, and a helping hand to your community. You give support and a listening ear to your friends, and a cheerful expression to all the people that cross your path every day.

And what do you receive? Strong families, supportive relationships, a safe community, and enjoyable friends.

You receive something back, but it's not always what you give, is it? You may give service and receive a paycheck. You may provide encouragement and receive gratitude.

So what do you think? Is it more important to give or receive?

It's not *either/or!* To lead a great business and a great life, you need to give *and* receive. The important issue here relates to sequence and quantity. Of course, you first *give* and then you *receive*. You *reap* after you've *sown*.

But sometimes, you may not want what you get back. You may give loyalty to a friend and get betrayal or you may give advice to a spouse and get resentment. Your harvest depends on many factors: the quality of the seed, the soil, the weather, and timing, to name a few.

> *Giving people a little more than they expect is a good way to get back a lot more than you'd expect.*
>
> *– ROBERT HALF*

Other times (and we believe that this is more the rule than the reverse) you give and you get back a lot more of what you want. Your business provides a service and you get paid for the service plus enough extra to make a profit. You give a listening ear to a friend, and the friend surprises you with a birthday party. You give encouragement to your loved ones, and they give you back a lifetime of gratitude.

Giving: Where Supply Exceeds Demand

Here's the good news: you reap *more* than you sow. You don't get back what you put in, you get *more.* Ask the owner of an orchard, vineyard or farm, or think of your experiences seeing barren fields in the winter and harvest fields in the fall.

This law of giving and receiving at first appears to be a law of simple, equal transactions. I give you something; I get something of equal value in return. But by observing thousands of successful people and hundreds of successful businesses over the last two decades, we've come to realize that the law of giving and receiving is not a zero sum game. It doesn't shake out in equal amounts of giving and receiving. There's abundance there, and it's constantly increasing.

If the majority of people of a country, no matter how great its natural resources, organize and conspire to get more out and put less in, to do less and get more, how long will, how long can *it last?*

– WILLIAM JH BOETCKER

For example, suppose I supply you with a service for washing your car. What I provide you (a car wash) is at least as valuable as the money you pay me for it, otherwise you wouldn't choose to have me wash it. On the other hand (assuming I run a profitable business), it costs me less than your fee to provide that service to you. The excess is my profit. I receive more than I give.

With that profit, I can now go purchase something of equal or greater value for myself that results, in turn, in a profit for someone else. They get more than they give. That little extra abundance—the profit—is what keeps on increasing. If I provide enough extra value for you, you'll come back for more. And so with every giving and receiving act, extra value is created. Get enough of these transactions going, and you have a healthy economy flowing.

The same is true on the personal level. Once you get enough goodwill going between people, it keeps on increasing. You love your children more, your spouse more. Your friends trust you more. You bring greater service to your community and place of worship.

The law of giving and receiving does not state that demand and supply are equal. It says that supply exceeds demand. Mr. K started with $5,000 and created millions for his investors and employees. Give and you get even more back—overflowing, abundant supply.

Giving from an Unlimited Supply

Some of our most valuable assets are things that we simply cannot run out of. There is always an ample supply of patience, wisdom, intelligence and kindness. Why? Because these qualities are not limited by anything physical. And the more we give away these things, the more they flow into our lives.

The same is true for customers, family members, friends, or associates. Giving wisely generates a cycle of increasing abundance.

Giving multiplies where it is valued. The more value, the more giving multiplies, and the more giving multiplies, the more value it creates. An endless, upward turning cycle.

Leadership Fundamental #2: How to Work with People

Joe: Stephen Covey has taught me much in our 14-year association. Few things, however, have been as far-reaching as the power of principles. Principles are universal truths, natural laws that produce predictable outcomes. Like gravity, principles exist everywhere, have always existed, and operate whether we understand them or not.

> *Win-win is a belief in the third alternative. It's not your way or my way; it's a better way, a higher way.*
>
> *– STEPHEN R. COVEY*

There is a fundamental principle that governs all human interactions. Effective, long-term relationships must be based on Win-Win. Not Win-Lose. Not Lose-Win. Certainly not Lose-Lose. There are, therefore, three ways to work with people.

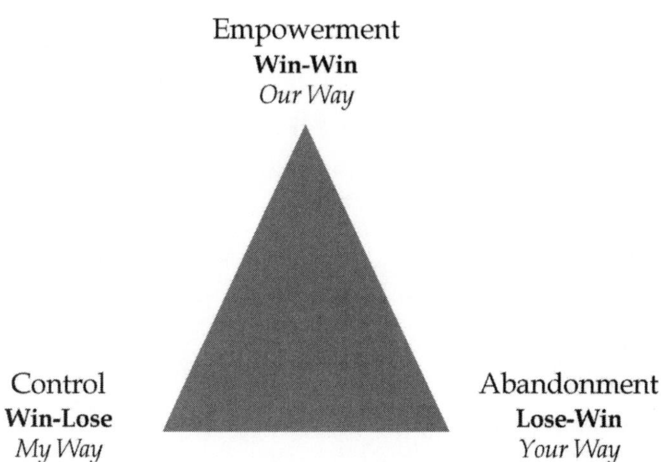

These three ways of dealing with people help us understand and apply this fundamental leadership principle.

In 1990, I endeavored to apply this Win-Win principle in all areas of my life. I'm embarrassed to admit this, but my tendency is to control. This is especially true when I find myself trying to "manage" others.

> *The measure of a man is what he does with power.*
>
> *– PITTACUS*

One of my first endeavors to apply Win-Win was with my seven-year-old son. My wife Diane and I were frustrated because we couldn't get Joseph to clean his room. Utilizing "the carrot and the stick" was not producing the results we were looking for. I remember walking into his room one day saying, "Joseph, if you clean your room, I'll take you out for some frozen yogurt" (carrot). Thirty minutes later, I came back and he had done nothing, so I went for the stick: "Joseph, you'd better get this room cleaned or I'll spank your little butt." Thirty minutes later, he'd done nothing. The spanking seemed extreme in this instance, so I went for abandonment: "You know, Joseph, if you don't want to clean your room, that's your business, but don't come crying to me when you can't find your soccer clothes."

Control creates dependency and kills the human spirit. Abandonment creates independence and severs relationships. Only Empowerment creates ownership, responsibility, and interdependence.

I wanted to maintain, even strengthen my relationship with Joseph while producing positive results—a clean room. On second thought, I really wanted much more—I wanted him to be able to lead his own life more effectively. Slowly but surely, my thinking was changing, and so were my behaviors.

Remember, we learn nothing by speaking.
– UNKNOWN

One day I asked Joseph, "What's my job?" He replied, "To take care of me, Daddy." "No," I said. "My real job is to teach you to take care of yourself." After a couple months, we both began to get it. Frankly, he caught on a little quicker than I did.

Some time later, I tried to considerately practice the advice of St. Francis of Assisi (later popularized as Habit 5 by Stephen R. Covey): "Seek first to understand, then to be understood."

"What are your dreams for the future?" I asked this grade-schooler.

"Dad, I've got it figured out," he said. "I'm going to live in a great big castle with my best friends. There will be a moat around it, and no girls allowed." (He's 20 now. The vision is different.) He said, "We're going to invent this little thing." He cupped his hands together, as if he could hold it. "That's going to power the entire world."

"Great!" I replied with genuine enthusiasm. "How big is this castle going to be?"

"Huge! It'll have about 50 rooms with all kinds of stuff."

"Wonderful! Now, what's my job?"

"To teach me to take care of myself," he said.

"Well then, I guess I'd better teach you how to take care of one room so that some day you'll know how to take care of 50."

He said, "Sure, Dad."

When we change our *thinking,* our *behaviors* change, and so do our *results.*

About three years later, I walked into my 10-year-old's bedroom, and he had emptied his closet and drawers of all contents and placed them on the bedroom floor. I remember thinking he'd gone into spontaneous regression.

> *Power can be seen as power* with *rather than power* over, *and it can be used for competence and cooperation rather than dominance and control.*
>
> – *ANNE L. BARSTOW*

"Joseph, what are you doing?" I asked, as my voice cracked nervously.

"Dad, I'm rearranging my room."

"Great! Let me show you how to do it," I replied (reverting back to a control style we both understood all too well).

"Dad," he replied, "I don't want to do it your way, I want to do it my way."

In that moment, we were experiencing the fruit of honest communication and interdependence. He pushed back, and I received it.

The final test of a leader is that he leaves behind in others the conviction and the will to carry on.

– WALTER LIPPMANN

I humbly asked, "Can I help?"

He said, "Sure. Fold that underwear up and put it in that drawer."

It was his room. It was his responsibility.

Last weekend, my wife visited Joseph at his second-year college apartment. She told me the place was immaculate.

So, how are you working with the people in your life? Effective long-term relationships require win-win thinking and win-win behaviors to achieve win-win results.

Leadership Fundamental #3: Two Types of Leaders

In our experience, high-performing companies are good at integrating two ways of looking at the enterprise. These two views of what's important are often individualized in two types of leaders: the Visionary Leader and the Operational Leader. A high-performing organization (or a declining one trying to revitalize itself), needs to be led by someone with great vision, a person that sees tremendous possibilities, a leader who can detect opportunities. Visionary Leaders communicate passionately and bring an extraordinary amount of energy and commitment to the work. They

> *Entrepreneurs are marked by the ability to paint a vision ...managers tend to be more 'down to earth.' Their work translates the visions of the entrepreneur into...performance. Entrepreneurial and managerial talents must be brought within a single harness if an organization is to succeed over time in a rapidly changing environment.*
>
> – JAMES M. STROCK

create a tremendous spirit of enthusiasm and positive momentum.

Often, these leaders are great at gathering people, commitment, and passion to an enterprise, but they are not so great at establishing procedures, working out processes, nor ensuring that the work being done is thorough, complete, and accurate.

Those are the things in which an Operational Leader excels. Operational Leaders bring efficiency, order, clarity, and process improvement. They're often brought in by Visionary Leaders to bring order out of chaos. They're good with details, numbers, procedures, routines, and speed.

So how do these two leadership styles work together? In many organizations, they don't. There is conflict.

Leaders do not avoid, repress or deny conflict, but rather see it as an opportunity. Once everyone has come to see it that way, they can exchange their combative posture for a creative stance, because they don't feel threatened, they feel challenged.

– WARREN BENNIS

Visionary Leaders may see Operational Leaders as being bureaucratic, as people that see only obstacles instead of opportunities. To the Visionary Leader, the Operational Leader holds the organization back from accomplishing all the possibilities that the visionary leader can see.

Operational Leaders often view Visionary Leaders as flighty, inconsistent, and as having lots of energy with no follow-through. An Operational Leader would love to build a strong business for the Visionary, if the Visionary could just decide what business he or she wants to be in!

We've seen it happen in so many organizations, we're tempted to call it a law: The Law of Conflict between the Visionary Leader and the Operational Leader.

It doesn't have to be this way, and in high-performing organizations, it's not. There, Visionary Leaders and Operational Leaders realize how valuable the other style of leadership is to the enterprise. There's a strong, consistent respect for the other's perspective and a real reaching out to accommodate the other's strengths and to minimize the other's weaknesses.

Visionary Leadership with Operational Leadership is not an "either/or" proposition. It's about "and" and "then." Notice the relationship between them on the following chart:

Visionary Leadership	then	Operational Leadership
Doing the Right Things	then	Doing More Things Faster
The Compass	then	The Clock
Clarify Direction	then	Execute Priorities

We had to learn this for ourselves, with Joe being the Visionary Leader and Bruce being the Operational Leader.

> *Only those who respect the personality of others can be of real use to them.*
>
> –*ALBERT SCHWEITZER*

For the first nine months of our initial business venture, the frustration was intense. Joe couldn't settle on a consistent business model, and Bruce couldn't adjust to the fast-changing nature of the small business world.

Once we figured out that we both needed the other's leadership talents, the results that we produced went through the roof. Sales went up, productivity went up, free time went up, and fun went up. Joe had to learn to trust Bruce's ability to run the day-to-day aspects of the business and Bruce had to learn to flow with Joe's intuition and business savvy.

The danger we faced was that we tended to personalize the conflict rather than see the conflict as two styles that needed to complement each other. When we broke through that barrier, productivity soared.

As you develop your business, you will need the right balance of Visionary and Operational Leaders.

Leadership Fundamental #4: The Purpose of a Business

According to studies funded by Harvard Business School, businesses that focus obsessively on meeting the needs of customers, employees and owners while developing leadership at all levels, outperform comparison companies in four critical areas:

- Revenues increase 4 times faster
- Job creation is 7 times greater
- Owner equity grows 12 times faster
- Profit performance is 750 times higher.

It's not really rocket science, is it? Leading a superb business may be a lot of hard work, but it's really not very complicated at its core. The purpose of a business is to:

- Serve Customers
- Serve Employees
- Serve Owners
- Develop Leaders at all levels

Or, as Stephen R. Covey writes in *Principle-Centered Leadership®*, the Universal Mission Statement is, "To improve the economic well-being and quality of life for all stakeholders."

Balancing the needs of these stakeholder groups is the key. To try to meet the needs of one stakeholder at the expense of the other two is not a healthy approach to leading a business. If you try to just meet the owners' needs (such as focusing only on making money), what happens to the customer and the employee? The customer will no longer believe that the company is looking out for his or her welfare. The employee starts to see the work only in terms of financial gain or job experience, not what they can contribute.

> *Anyone who says they work just for the money has given up the hope that anything more is possible.*
>
> – *PETER BLOCK*

Later on, we'll show you how to write a plan that meets the needs of your primary stakeholders. You'll want to define your objectives and strategies for customers, employees, and owners and create ways to measure your progress. This way, you can be sure that you're balancing their needs and making progress.

Leadership Fundamental #5: The Wisdom of 80/20

You know the deal:

- 20% of the people have 80% of the wealth.
- 80% of a book's value can be found in 20% of the pages.
- 20% of your clothes will be worn 80% of the time.
- 20% of your customers give you 80% of your profits (or headaches).

Of course, it's not always exactly 80/20. Sometimes it's more like 80/1.3 (80% of movie revenues come from 1.3% of the movies produced). The point is, as Richard Koch writes in his book *The 80/20 Principle,* "...there is an inbuilt imbal-

> *Things that matter most should never be at the mercy of things that matter least.*
>
> – *JOHANN GOETHE*

ance between causes and results, inputs and outputs, and effort and reward."

This principle is so fundamental it's like a Swiss army knife—it can help in lots of different situations. The question is, how can we use it to leverage the highest results?

There are two major ways this rule can help us. It can teach us what to focus on (the 20%) and what to eliminate or reduce (the 80%).

For example, are we really short on time? If the 80/20 rule holds true, then we accomplish 80% of our results in about 20% of our time. If we could accomplish all the things we're doing during that 20% in a single day, we'd get almost a week's worth of work done on Monday. If we could repeat that, we'd get another 80% of our normal results on Tuesday. *That would get us 160% productivity in 40% of the time!* If we really get this, and have the management skills to make it happen, we would never have a shortage of time to do the 20% things. And *we would stop seeing time as a scarce commodity.* The 80/20 Principle gives us more time.

If in fact we achieve 80% of our results in 20% of our time, then the converse is also true, 80% of our time is spent achieving 20% of our results. Does this give us some help in identifying what work we might consider eliminating?

Apply the 80/20 rule to your team. If your whole team is spending 80% of it's time to get 20% of its results, don't you suppose there's some work in there that could be eliminated or reduced? Do you think investing a little bit of time to eliminate a lot of unnecessary work would be helpful? Of course it would! The key to using the 80/20 rule is to focus on the few activities that generate the most results. *The 80/20 rule shows us what to eliminate or reduce.*

Bruce: One of our clients installs heating and air conditioning units in new homes. When the owners started the company, they did all the work themselves—measuring the job, cutting the sheet metal, installing the ductwork and the equipment. They worked hard, they worked fast, and they did great work.

They knew they could get more done if they trained others to do this work, so they started doing that. One of the owners focused on selling, one on training workers in the metal shop. After a few years, they grew their revenue to a couple of million a year.

They still continued to grow, so once again, they had to focus on what they did best, where they could contribute the most value. They saw that they needed to start training trainers and managers, so they focused on that. The 80/20 rule helps us focus on how we can multiply what we give.

> *If we did realize the difference between the vital few and the trivial many in all aspects of our lives and if we did something about it, we could multiply anything that we valued.*
>
> – *RICHARD KOCH*

Now 14 years after starting their business, they are the largest of their type in their city, grossing over $20 million in sales.

Have they quit using the 80/20 rule? Not at all. They continue to seek ways to leverage their time and attention on the activities that will have the biggest impact, delegating the rest to other people or choosing not to pursue certain activities at all.

One more example. This client operates by three values they stick to vigorously: Show up on time. Do quality work. Charge a fair price. Three values on which they built their great reputation and prosperous business. The 80/20 principle can help you clarify your most important values.

How else could we apply the 80/20 rule to focus our business products and services? To target training and development efforts? To serve customers? To select vendors? To establish individual priorities?

Later on, in the section, The First Practice: Clarify, we demonstrate how to use this fundamental tool for analyzing company strengths, weaknesses, opportunities and threats otherwise known as "S.W.O.T." We use the S.W.O.T. process to help refine our understanding and articulation of strategies and priorities.

Besides the noble art of getting things done, there is the noble art of leaving things undone. The wisdom of life consists in the elimination of nonessentials.

– LIN YU TANG

The great thing about the 80/20 principle is that it will always be in operation. If you were to apply the 80/20 principle to your personal productivity, you might find yourself a year from now being 50% more productive than you are now. Would you still be accomplishing 80% of your results in about 20% of your time? Undoubtedly. The 80/20 principle will *always* be there to help you prune your efforts to produce the best results. With it, you can always find the few things which will cause a significant difference. *Focus there. Reduce the rest.*

Leadership Fundamental #6: Clarify and Simplify

Things get complicated without any effort on our part. This is especially true in business.

Others make it complicated. Vendor shipments don't include the right parts. Tax laws change. Clients ask for exceptions. Employees ask for special considerations. Your family needs you to take a Thursday off. And we make it complicated.

> *You can't believe how hard it is for people to be simple, how much they fear being simple. They worry that if they're simple, people will think they're simpleminded. In reality, of course, it's just the reverse.*
>
> – *JACK WELCH*

If you're a Visionary Leader you see possibilities everywhere. Every month (or week) you want to launch a new venture. There's a wonderful opportunity to serve a new market or customer.

If you're an Operational Leader, you want to change the system, restructure, reorganize, and put new procedures into place.

Suddenly, what looked like a simple, straightforward enterprise is now filled with complexity, confusion, uncertainty, and chaos.

So what do you do? Clarify and simplify. That's it! Clarify and simplify. To clarify and simplify becomes the rhythm of your leadership.

- So what do you need to get clear and simple about?
- Company *aspiration*: Vision, mission, and values
- Company *objectives*: How you're doing by the numbers
- *Strategies*: What paths you've decided to take and why
- *Priorities*: What each individual's contribution is expected to be

A great tool for getting this down on paper is your One Page Strategic Plan. Getting your business plan on one page (without shrinking fonts or margins!) is a wonderful way to reach a clear and simple understanding of what your business is all about.

> *Business plans don't have to be complex and cumbersome.*
>
> – *JIM HORAN*

We'll be walking you through the step-by-step process of building a business plan in Section 3, Clarify Direction. For now, it's important to realize that clarifying and simplifying must be a part of the way you approach your business world. Don't oversimplify; you don't want to discount or dismiss important considerations. Take the complex and make it simple enough for people to take action.

You can see how Leadership Fundamental #5, The Wisdom of 80/20, can be useful here. The 20% of your effort that produces 80% of your results is a good place to start making things simpler. What are the few things that produce the most results? Those few become your key to making business and life simpler and clearer.

Who wouldn't want to be leading or working for an organization with that level of clarity and simplicity?

PART

2

The First Practice: CLARIFY

The Problem with Planning

There are three problems with planning:

- It takes too much time
- It costs too much money
- It has minimal impact

Other than that—no problem!

Here's a typical planning experience. An executive team meets offsite, perhaps in an exotic location, for several days of strategic planning. There's a lot of talk, mostly from just a few people. There's a lot of positioning with each executive trying to protect their department from being beat up too badly. Finally, there's some agreement on who's going to be responsible for what.

> *No involvement, no commitment.*
>
> *– STEPHEN R. COVEY*

A few days afterwards, a large document in a three-ring binder arrives on each executive's desk. It's the strategic plan, and it's already out of date. It goes on a shelf, and there it sits until the first performance review session some months later.

No wonder most executive teams dread the planning process.

There is a better way. Here are the guidelines:

1. Instead of taking several days, invest one day to clarify the essential elements: vision, mission, values, objectives, strategies, and priorities.
2. When conducting your planning workshop, use group processes that allow for each person's input and the taking of the group's pulse as a whole.
3. Instead of a complex, thick document that sits on a shelf, put a clear and simple plan on one page.
4. Even more, instead of producing a document that's out of date as soon as it's printed, use an online "document" or web page that each person can keep updated in real time (see **www. prioritize.com**).
5. Write your priorities in clear, compelling language.

I wouldn't give a fig for the simplicity on this side of complexity; I would give my right arm for the simplicity on the far side of complexity.

– OLIVER WENDALL HOLMES

(For a sample strategic plan that fits on one page, see page 58.)

The Simple Solution: *Prioritize!*

It only helps so much to know what can go wrong. What's better is to know how to do it right. So here it is. People who build great companies:

- Clarify Direction
- Execute Priorities
- Renew the Spirit

> *We think in generalities, but we live in detail.*
>
> –ALFRED NORTH WHITEHEAD

These are the three practices of *Prioritize!* and the topics for the middle sections of this book. Here is a brief overview:

Clarify

This is determining the path of the organization, clarifying the three things an organization needs if it is to be successful:

- Where the organization is going (long-term)

- How the organization is going to get there (mid-term)
- What the work is that needs to be done now (short-term)

These three clarifications indicate three time frames: "where" is the long-term, "how" is the mid-term, and "what" is the short-term.

Execute

Once the direction is determined, you have to make progress. People have already defined their top priorities as they Clarify Direction, so now they need to execute those priorities. You'll want to track what is getting done, what barriers are getting in the way, and what the next steps are. Progress review meetings, measuring results, and taking appropriate action makes up the substance of moving an organization forward.

> *We first make our habits, then our habits make us.*
>
> *– UNKNOWN*

Renew

If there's one thing we're sure of, it's that things will change. Markets, employees, owners, products, technology, and the economy—they all change. For us to serve effectively, we have to adjust to the changes going on around us.

Building on our foundation of Leadership Fundamentals (Give, then Receive; Working with People; Visionary Leaders and Operational Leaders; the Purpose of a Business; the Wisdom of 80/20; Clarify and Simplify) you're ready to launch into the first practice of *Prioritize!*: Clarify.

The One Page Strategic Plan

A One Page Strategic Plan has six elements: vision, mission, values, objectives, strategies, and priorities:

> *The best way to predict your future is to create it.*
>
> – *STEPHEN R. COVEY*

- ***Vision***: a clear picture of your destination
- ***Mission***: the driving purpose of your business
- ***Values***: the guidelines you use for decision making and how you treat each other
- ***Objectives***: the numbers you track
- ***Strategies:*** *the paths you've decided to take*
- ***Priorities***: the work that needs to be done now and who needs to do it

The first five elements are common to your entire team, but priorities are individualized.

We've rarely seen a business plan that was too short. We have seen hundreds that would make an acceptable cure for insomnia. Here's the good news, we have never encountered an organization that couldn't fit their plan on one page. Sure, you have to cut out a lot of verbiage, but getting the plan on one page forces you to become really clear about what's important.

Your imagination is your preview of life's coming attractions.

– DENIS WAITLEY

Imagine the power that a simple clear plan will give you and your people. It cuts through complexity, arranges issues in order of importance, streamlines decision-making, defines success, and measures progress. People know what they're supposed to accomplish, see how their work supports the bigger picture, and can easily determine the impact if their priorities need to change.

Everything should be made as simple as possible, but not simpler.

– ALBERT EINSTEIN

Our experience has demonstrated that any enterprise can achieve extraordinary results by developing, executing, and adjusting their One Page Strategic Plan. The following sections give you simple and clear guidelines for defining these six elements of your plan while involving the right people in this process. We'll start by showing you how these six elements fall clearly into three distinct time frames: long-term (five years or more), mid-term (one to three years), and short-term (this quarter).

Let's start with an example of a crisp strategic plan:

One Page Strategic Plan Guidelines

Vision	What is our ideal future? • What will we provide to whom, and on what type of scale? • Is it clear and inspiring?
Mission	Why do we exist? What's our purpose? • Will it fit on a t-shirt? • Can you recite it as fast as your phone number? • Does it explain why we do what we do?
Values	What will guide our decisions and conduct? • Are there five or fewer?
Objectives	How will we measure progress? • What are our key measures? • Are we measuring customer satisfaction, employee satisfaction, and financial success? • Are they simple?
Strategies	How will we get to our vision? • What paths will we take? • What are the categories we will use to organize action? (Marketing, innovation, human resources, financial resources, physical resources, productivity, social responsibility, and profit requirements)
Priorities	What needs to be done in the next 90 days? • Are priorities assigned to individuals? • Do they start with a verb, end with a date, and have something measurable in between? • Do priorities connect to strategies?

Sample One Page Strategic Plan for Bobtronics, Inc.

Vision	Bobtronics will be the premier provider of bobolators to the international electronics industry.
Mission	Smaller machines for a better world.
Values	Respect, integrity, fairness, fun
Objectives	22% growth, 10% profit, 95% customer retention, 80% employee satisfaction
Strategies	• Human Resources: Release our people's innovation through training and incentives. • Innovation: Create new versions of the bobolator for use in new industries. • Marketing: Raise awareness of bobolators through broad-based marketing, media interviews, and science journal articles. • Sales: Increase revenue over last year by penetrating the bio-tech industry. • Operations: Increase operational efficiencies through technology, industry best practices, and process improvement.
Priorities	• Add new distributor for bio-tech by 5/30. • Fill CFO position by 5/15. • Get new IS system online by 6/30. • Pick gain-sharing option by 4/30. • Add new sales mgr by 6/15.

The Three Time Frames of Planning

When Clarifying Direction, it's useful to think in terms of three time frames:

- Long-Term Aspirations—where your organization is going
- Mid-Term Objectives and Strategies—How you're going to get there.
- Short-Term Priorities—What needs to be done now.

> *The way you view the future influences what you do today and what you do today influences the future.*
>
> *—DAN BURRUS*

Aspirations are long-term, usually five, 10, or 25 years out. They include your vision, mission, and values. These elements provide the stable core around which everything else flows. What kind of business you're trying to build (Vision), why you're building it (Mission), and how you're going to treat each other along the way (Values)—these all tend to be timeless and foundational to all other choices.

Objectives are mid-term. They're like mile markers along the way. They are the measurements to help you track your progress as an organization. How fast, how big, how far do you want to go in terms of customer satisfaction, employee satisfaction, revenue or any other key indicator of success?

Strategies are also mid-term, usually one to three years out. In the wilderness of business, there are many paths to take. In marketing, for example, will you choose direct mail, email campaigns, print advertising, broadcast media, referrals, or convention booths? Strategies are the choices you make about which paths are best.

Priorities are short-term, usually accomplished within 90 days. Once you've chosen your strategies and objectives, you identify the work that needs to get done now. High-performance emerges when a powerful vision is coupled with execution.

Defining a simple long-term vision 10-25 years out and deciding on a handful of priorities for the next quarter are the two most important decisions a business leader makes.

– VERNE HARRISH

In his book, *Mastering the Rockefeller Habits,* Verne Harnish relates some lessons learned from GE's Jack F. Welch Leadership Center. "In planning, the 'middle' is gone. You only have to define two points: where you plan to be 10 to 25 years from now and what you have to do in the next 90 days. You don't want to fall in love with your own one to three year plans." You still need the mid-term to help choose your priorities; the point is, don't get stuck on them because they'll change.

To get going in the right direction, we need to start with the long-term. Vision comes first.

3 Time Frames and 6 Essential Elements of a 1-Page Strategic Plan
I. Long-Term Aspirations
1. Vision
2. Mission
3. Values
N
W
E
S
5-25 Years
II. Mid-Term
4. Objectives
5. Strategies
1-3 Years
90 Days
III. Short-Term
6. Priorities with Action Plans
Current Realities SWOT Analysis
You Are Here!

Vision

The 1950's and 60's featured several visionaries on the national stage. President Kennedy proclaimed, "We will take a man to the moon and return him to earth safely by the end of the decade. We do it, not because it is easy, but because it is hard." Martin Luther King, Jr. declared, "I have a dream that my four little children will one day live in a nation where they will be judged not by the color of their skin, but by the content of their character."

> *Of all the things I've done, the most vital is coordinating the talents of those who work for us and pointing them toward a certain goal.*
>
> – *WALT DISNEY*

In his book *Deliberate Success*, Eric Allenbaugh writes, "King and other visionary leaders did not declare: 'I have a strategic plan!' No, they each promoted a compelling vision that touched the hearts and souls of others. They effectively engaged others in transforming the dream into reality. That's what visionary leadership is all about!"

Vision is a desired future state. As Burt Nanus has said, "A vision is only an idea or an image of a more desirable future for the organization, but the right vision is an idea so energizing that it in effect jump-starts the future by calling forth the skills, talents, and resources to make it happen."

Here are the four basic elements of a useful vision statement:

1. What business you're in
2. What products and services you offer
3. Who you're trying to serve
4. The scope of operations (local to global).

Here is an example from Apple Computer: "Apple is committed to bring the best personal computing products and support to students, educators, designers, scientists, engineers, business persons and consumers in over 140 countries around the world."

Strive for excellence, not perfection.
– H.JACKSON BROWN, JR.

Visions serve best when they have an inspiring element while not going overboard. Apple's aspiration to provide the "best" products and support offer that inspirational element.

It's easy to see that if the top leaders in an organization don't agree on at least these four elements, it will be difficult to move in the same direction.

But once you've gotten this much clear, it releases people to think creatively about how they're going to get there.

One of our clients was recently considering the expansion of their automobile business. Our first exercise was to ask each member of the executive team to write down the number of locations they wanted to be operating within five years. All but one individual wrote "3" on their card. The other person wrote some really big number, like "20." Needless to say, the shared vision was clear. As of this writing, their profits have doubled as they successfully operate in their second location. The third location is on the drawing board.

> *The voyage of discovery is not in seeing new landscapes but in having new eyes.*
>
> *–MARCEL PROUST*

Vision is a clear picture of your destination. It answers questions like these:

- Where are you going?
- What are you trying to build?
- What will it look like when you get there?

The keys to writing a vision are:

1. Invest enough time, but not too much time in the process.
2. Involve the right people in the process.
3. Integrate the best ideas of each contributor over time. This is a process, not an event.

We have participated in (and facilitated, we're sorry to say) day-long executive sessions devoted solely to creating vision, mission and values statements. The results are often bland and uninspiring after we've compromised the life out of them. Today, our clients are getting better results in one-fourth the time.

It doesn't have to be extremely difficult if you use the "Good Enough" rule: if you feel like it's Good Enough, you're probably right. Go ahead and create the initial draft of your plan. Further reflection, experience, and inspiration will help you refine it at a future date.

Mission

Mission is purpose. It defines your reason for being, your motivation for being in the marketplace. It should be short, clear, memorable, and compelling.

Peter Drucker tells the story of a group of healthcare professionals who developed a mission statement for the emergency room that read, "Our mission is healthcare." Short? Yes, but not so clear and compelling.

> *It does not require many words to speak the truth.*
>
> – CHIEF JOSEPH

After further discussion, the administrators acknowledged that the emergency room does not take care of health; it takes care of illness or injury. After talking about it more, they realized that many people who come to the emergency room need assurance, not medical treatment.

They realized that the real purpose of the emergency room was to give patients and their loved ones *assurance*, even if they couldn't give them immediate health. So they created this mission—"To give assurance to the afflicted."

He who has a 'why' to live for can bear with almost any 'how'.
– FRIEDRICH NIETZSCHE

Now, with this mission, the first objective for nurses and doctors is to see every new patient within one minute of their arrival, to give assurance.

"To give assurance to the afflicted." Short, clear, *and* compelling.

Drucker also suggests that you put your mission to the T-shirt test. Can it fit on a T-shirt? Is it eight words or less? Does it describe why your organization exists? Does it provide direction for doing the right things?

Here's an example from Federal Express:

"The World on Time."

If you can't recite your mission as quickly as your phone number, then it's too long. Keep at it. You can get there. Clarify and simplify.

Values

Values do two things for your enterprise:

- They guide your decisions.
- They're a contract for how you treat each other.

Lou Holtz is recognized as one of America's most successful football coaches. He has never taken over a winning college team. Yet within two years, every one of his teams has played in a Bowl game. Many attribute his success and the character of his players to his core values—do what's right, do your best, treat others as you want to be treated.

> *Values are the bedrock of any corporate culture.*
>
> *– TERRENCE E. DEAL & ALLEN A. KENNEDY*

Living with a set of core values can be very difficult. Living without them is even worse. So, let's take up some issues regarding values.

Living with values can be difficult. Once you put a set of values in front of your people, you immediately run the risk of being hypocritical. Why? Because it is so easy to justify not following them. And if there's one way to kill the credibility of your leadership, it's to violate your own values.

One of our clients recently identified "honesty" as a shared value. A short time later, one of the executives asked a fellow employee to be dishonest in a transaction. The story spread like wildfire and dramatically undermined the executive's credibility. Not surprisingly, this executive was asked to leave the organization. He was de-hired.

If I take care of my character, my reputation will take care of itself.

– DWIGHT LYMAN MOODY

Living without them is even worse. Without a code of conduct, anything goes. The media provides a steady stream of the most recent businesses where leadership has gone awry. We could all point to similar cases in government, non-profits, churches, educational institutions, and communities. Organizations are destroyed, careers ended, families ruined because no values were in place to guide decisions and conduct.

You don't know what your values are worth until you know how much you're willing to pay for them. If you hold a value of open, honest communication, what are you willing to pay to uphold that value? The discomfort of confronting a colleague (or boss or owner) on an issue? The loss of your next career advancement? Your job itself? As an owner, what's a value worth when it might cost you your biggest customer?

So, when you identify your values, make sure they're really your values!

Values are shared through stories. A set of values is fine-tuned over time, and the best way to communicate what your values mean in your workplace is to share stories. These stories should always illustrate how a value was demonstrated or violated. The body of stories you tell each other strengthens the collective understanding of how to live out your values.

At the Air Force Academy, for example, the honor code—"We will not lie, steal, or cheat nor tolerate among us anyone who does"—is taught through the use of real-life situations of cadet stories—cadets who were suspected of violating the honor code. These anonymous stories are shared on a regular basis with the entire student body. Over time, a deep understanding develops in how to apply the core values of honesty and trustworthiness.

> *Know your truth, speak your truth, live your truth.*
>
> *– EILEEN HANNEGAN*

Finding your values. One way to help you identify your values is to make a list of people in your organization that model the values you would like to see demonstrated by everyone. Then ask, what are the four or five qualities, traits or behaviors that these people embody? That list will be your values.

Values tend to be more universal than personal. Sure, people may have differences in *taste* (I like blue, you like green). But people tend to share the same *values*. Research done at the Institute for Global Ethics shows a nearly universal agreement with five primary values: honesty, respect, responsibility, fairness, and compassion. If you're having trouble creating a set of values, you wouldn't be far off if you started with these.

Decision-making becomes smoother and faster with a well-defined set of values. Values inform who you should hire (and fire), how you reward people, and how you treat suppliers, customers, and your community. Values become the substance of your company culture, the stories you tell about each other, especially when you bring new people into your organization. Once the values are clear, decision-making becomes easier for every level in the organization.

Here's one final thought on Aspirations—they don't need to be limited to Vision, Mission, and Values. One of our clients, a regional leader in payroll processing, elected to add a *Foundation*—"To honor God in all we do." Ritz-Carlton Basics includes a *Motto*—"We are ladies and gentlemen serving ladies and gentlemen."

Other organizations include Cornerstones, Principles, Philosophies, etc. All of these statements provide a long-term compass and clarify direction over the long term.

Objectives

In 1953, three percent of Harvard Graduates had a set of written goals. Twenty years later, those individuals had achieved more in terms of financial success than the other 97% *combined*. It's been our experience that the same effect is true for organizations—organizations with clear objectives consistently outperform organizations without clear objectives. We may have noble Aspirations and compelling Strategies, but Objectives provide the way to measure high-performance.

> *Too often we measure everything and understand nothing. The three most important things you need to measure in a business are customer satisfaction, employee satisfaction, and cash flow.*
>
> *–JACK WELCH*

When we talk about Objectives, we're talking about measuring the progress of your organizational performance. Often, that means numbers: financials, customer loyalty, employee engagement. Objectives tell us what your goals are in reaching certain levels of performance in key business areas.

So how's your business doing? It could be difficult for you to answer this question without some measurements.

Suppose you are going on a journey. If I ask you how your trip is going, you might share with me some of the fun you've been having and what you've been learning. If I want to know about the progress you're making in reaching your destination, you might tell me you're in western Kansas. But in order for me to know what that means, I'd have to first know where you wanted to be. Did you want to be in Tennessee or Utah? Objectives define where you want to be at any given point in time.

Management by objectives works if you know the objectives.

– PETER DRUCKER

Picking the right numbers to track for your business is one of the most important decisions you can make, because as Michael LeBoeuf writes, "People do what gets measured."

Here are some principles for defining objectives:

Keep the objectives simple. If you have complicated measurements, you will get complicated systems.

Objectives should balance each other. This way you prevent the tendency to make one number look good at the expense of another. If you measure customer satisfaction, be sure to measure employee satisfaction, since one of these can be achieving by sacrificing the other. Of course, well-balanced objectives address the needs of customers, employees and owners.

Whenever possible, graph your numbers. If you set them up correctly, graphs will give you information more clearly than a table of numbers or a paragraph of words (for a powerful example of graphing, see Measuring Progress I: Tracking Results).

High-performing companies set Objectives, communicate them frequently, and let team members know how they're doing.

Why S.W.O.T.?

If your aspiration is to get to Rome, you'll want to know where you are now. Then and only then can you effectively strategize on how to get there. Doing a S.W.O.T. analysis is a powerful way to look at the brutal realities.

S.W.O.T. stands for Strengths, Weaknesses, Opportunities, and Threats. To get a clear picture of your current reality, look at both your internal realities (Strengths and Weaknesses) and external realities (Opportunities and Threats). It's a familiar tool to many, but many could use it to much greater advantage.

After doing a S.W.O.T. analysis, the strategies that map your path from where you are (S.W.O.T.) to where you want to be (vision, mission, values, and objectives) will be much easier to understand and articulate. The result of your S.W.O.T. analysis will be a clear and concise list of issues that you will want to address in your One Page Strategic Plan. This list will help define your path by improving the strategies and priorities that will help you get there. After sharpening your strategies and priorities in this way, circle back through your S.W.O.T. items and ensure that action is being taken on each high-leverage issue.

Opportunities are usually disguised by hard work so most people don't recognize them.

– ANN LANDERS

You will see from this process that our first practice of clarifying direction draws the map from where you are to where you want to be. That's why we start with vision, mission, values, and objectives. We start with where you want to be because it's easier to move an organization forward if we're future focused. If we *start* the process by defining where you are in your current situation, we tend to get problem-focused. However, as Jim Collins shows in his book, *Good to Great,* companies that achieve greatness have the wisdom to face the brutal realities. To see your current situation in the clear light of day you must do a S.W.O.T.

O.K. Now let's look at how to conduct an effective S.W.O.T. analysis.

How to Conduct a S.W.O.T. Analysis

If companies can waste hours creating Vision, Mission and Values statements, they waste *days* discussing current realities. There *is* a better way!

Here are three simple steps to identify your current realities.

- Assemble the right team
- Brainstorm using an Affinity Exercise
- Multi-vote to sort issues in order of importance

> *Leadership does not begin just with vision. It begins with getting people to confront the brutal facts and act on the implications.*
>
> – *JIM COLLINS*

The first step is to assemble a small group of leaders who understand the issues related to your customers, employees, owners, and other critical stakeholders.

The second step is to conduct what's called an Affinity Exercise.

An Affinity Exercise used in this fashion works somewhat like a brainstorm. Remind people of the rules of brainstorming: quantity matters more than quality; speed is good; don't stop to analyze or edit yourself.

Start with Strengths. Give everyone a pad of sticky notes and a felt tip pen. (You want to be able to see the writing from a few feet away.) Set a time limit of 1-2 minutes (you'll be surprised to learn you don't need any more time than this) and have everyone brainstorm a list of organizational Strengths, writing one Strength per sticky note. Just write the Strength on the note and put it aside. Write as many as you can in 60-120 seconds. Then call "Stop!"

Have everyone go to a wall and put their notes up in random order. Just get them up there. Then have everyone work together to arrange the notes by categories. Talk to each other. "I've got Expertise here, anybody else see anything related to that?"

There is a master key to success with which no man can fail. Its name is simplicity. Simplicity, I mean, in the sense of reducing to the simplest possible terms every problem that besets us.

– SIR HENRI DETERDING

In the end you'll have categories of notes together and perhaps a few orphans (strengths that have only one sticky note each). At this point you'll want to record the categories and orphans on a flip chart. Your list may include Great People, Good Management, Great Location, Good Communication, etc.

Now repeat the Affinity Exercise with Weaknesses, Opportunities, and Threats. At the end you will have four lists of issues on four separate flipchart pages.

Sure, there are some items that may show up on more than one list. Having a sole supplier for a critical component may be both a strength and a weakness.

In the end, it doesn't really matter on which list an issue shows up. The goal is to identify those issues you want to address strategically. You want to assign the issue as a priority for someone. So whether an issue is a weakness or a threat won't really matter. The categories are there to help stir thoughts so that the analysis of your Current Reality is complete.

Now for the third step: Multi-voting. Multi-voting is a way to quickly prioritize a list using everyone's input. Here's how it works:

First delete all the duplicate items; otherwise the votes will need to be combined later.

Count up the number of items remaining on all four lists. Let's say you have 35 items (eight Strengths, 10 Weaknesses, eight Opportunities, and nine Threats). Divide that number by three and round up. In this case you have 12.

The greatest thing in this world is not so much where we are, but in which direction we're moving.

– OLIVER WENDELL HOLMES

So everyone gets 12 votes. They can "spend" their votes any way they want, with one restriction: No more than three votes on any one item. So they could vote for four items by putting three votes on each or they could vote for 12 items by putting one vote on each, or any combination.

There's one criterion for voting. Choose only those items worthy of strategic consideration. It doesn't do you much good to identify the economy as a threat if you don't want to focus attention there.

Here's an important tip: have people write their votes down on a piece of paper before they start recording the votes on the flip chart. That way the first few people voting won't influence the other votes.

Then have everybody mark their votes on the flip charts and total the votes. After everyone has voted, there is usually a clear break between a few items that get a lot of votes and the many items that get few or no votes. Remember the 80/20 Principle?

Before you attempt to set things right, make sure you see things right.
– BLAINE LEE

You've just prioritized your S.W.O.T. issues and you've probably done it in less than an hour. Everyone has participated equally and so you have a strong sense of buy-in when it comes to taking action. Later, you'll review this list before finalizing everyone's Priorities. With a clear sense of where you are, you can plot your course to your vision. Plotting that course is the purpose of the next step, Strategies.

Strategies

Creating a set of strategies is like defining the route you're going to take on a trip. You make several high-level decisions about how you're going to get to your destination. Do you want to take the scenic route or the fastest route? Are there certain sites you want to see along the way? Will you be going by train or car or jet? Once your route is planned, many other decisions can be made.

> *The way to get good ideas is to get lots of ideas and throw the bad ones away.*
>
> – *LINUS PAULING*

A set of strategies should encompass all the high-leverage (80/20) issues that need to be addressed.

There are three steps to creating a set of strategies.

- Decide what areas in your business require strategic focus.
- Make some "big picture" choices.
- Write your strategies clearly and simply.

What areas of your business require strategic focus? The issues identified in your S.W.O.T. analysis may fit nicely into Peter Drucker's eight strategic categories: marketing, innovation, human resources, financial resources, physical resources, productivity, social responsibility and profit requirements. Or, you may choose other areas!

> *There is nothing so useless as doing efficiently that which should not be done at all.*
>
> – *PETER DRUCKER*

Make some "big picture" choices. These are the choices you make about how you want to lead and manage your business. For example, let's look at a marketing strategy. How will you attract customers? There are many possible paths: referrals; word of mouth; direct mail; giving speeches; advertising through radio, TV, or print media; e-mail, convention booths, and many more. Which ones will you choose? Those choices define your strategy.

Write your strategies in a clear format. Start with a verb, use *through* or *by*, and end with two to three bullet points. Here are some examples of well-written strategies:

- *Marketing:* Attract customers through referrals, direct mail, and radio ads.
- *Sales:* Generate revenue by training our distributors and focusing on the high-tech industry.
- *Innovation:* Launch new products through market research and competitive analysis.
- *Human Resources:* Develop our people to make significant contributions through identifying strengths, training, and mentoring.

- *Productivity:* Increase productivity through process improvement and acquiring new equipment.

Once you have a set of strategies in place, all other actions in the company can be aligned with them. If an activity is not aligned with a strategy, then you need to either eliminate the activity or rewrite your strategies to include what really needs to be done.

Priorities

Now we're at the heart of it all: Defining Priorities. Priorities translate strategy into results. As Peter Drucker says, "All grand strategies eventually deteriorate into work." Priorities are the primary tool to accomplish extraordinary results in any organization. After your planning is complete, your focus shifts to priorities alone. For execution, you don't refer to aspirations, objectives, or strategies very much. The focus will be on priorities and how much you're getting done. That's why defining the right priorities in a clear and simple way becomes absolutely critical.

> *The crime which bankrupts man and nations is that of turning aside from one's main purpose to serve a job here and there.*
>
> – *RALPH WALDO EMERSON*

Here are some guidelines for writing an effective priority:

Assign each priority to one person. Others may have supportive roles, but one person has primary ownership of each priority. This prevents the ancient problem: "Everybody thought Somebody was going to do it. Anybody could have done it. But Nobody did it."

Connect every priority to a strategy. If a priority doesn't help you implement a strategy, then one of two things are wrong: either you shouldn't be doing it or you haven't written your strategies broadly enough.

Describe an outcome or desired result. Priorities focus on results, not just activities. "Do accounting" doesn't tell you what needs to be done. It would clearer to say, "Publish monthly financial statements by the 25th of each month."

Start with a verb. The best verbs show finished actions. "Complete" is a good verb, while "manage" is not. "Make recommendations" is better than "research." "Publish" is better than "coordinate." Your goal is to get to clarity about what people are responsible for producing.

> *What may be done at any time will be done at no time.*
>
> *– SCOTTISH PROVERB*

End with a date. It's usually best to write priorities with a 90-day time frame in mind, although you can chose to make exceptions. Even if you have a project that will go beyond 90 days, you can still write a priority: "Complete 40% of new product launch project by December 31." Without dates, it's hard to organize your work. "As soon as possible" is not acceptable.

Make it measurable or observable. Most work can be quantified in some way as in, "Generate $350,000 in sales by March 31." But what if you can't predict the outcome? What if sales are not that predictable in your market? You can still write an effective priority—"Analyze my sales pipeline with my manager by the 5th of every month." You may not be able to predict your actual sales, but you should be able to produce information and get coaching on what's going on in your job.

Keep the number of priorities small. We think about five priorities is right. Fewer are o.k. Barnett Helzberg, founder of Helzberg Diamonds, one of the largest diamond retailers in the United States, once told us, "I guess I had five priorities: sell more diamonds, sell more diamonds, sell more diamonds, sell more diamonds, sell more diamonds." Helzberg's simple, focused approach was undoubtedly a key to his success.

Encouraging a team to write clear priorities is a very high-leverage leadership activity. When your people are clear about what they're responsible for producing, their efforts become more focused and their time usage improves.

Action Plans

An Action Plan is so simple and so powerful.

If a Priority is like climbing a staircase, the Action Plan details the individual steps. Although action plans don't usually fit on a One Page Strategic Plan, they provide the necessary clarity to take action, manage one's time, and make progress.

> *The elevator to success is out of order. You'll have to use the stairs…one step at a time.*
>
> *–JOE GIRARD*

Here's how it works: Action Plans help us achieve Priorities, Priorities help us achieve Strategies, and Strategies help us achieve our Vision.

Let's show you an example:

Vision	To be the premier provider of liquid material handling equipment nationally.
Strategy	People: Get the right people in the right positions, develop their talent and manage them effectively.
Priority	Start new CFO by June 30.
Action items	☑ Advertise 3 times in Sunday paper by May 1. ☑ Contact 10 business associates for referrals by May 5. ☑ Pick final candidates for interviews by May 15. ☐ Complete interviews by June 1. ☐ Make offer by June 15. ☐ Welcome new CFO on the first day by June 30.

It's so easy to see progress just by glancing at the number of items that are checked off. The dates in an Action Plan are not always as critical as the date on a priority. (So what if you're a day or a week late in making the offer if the new CFO can still start by June 30?)

The immature mind hops from one thing to another, the mature mind seeks to follow through.
–HARRY A. OVERSTREET

Think what power and imagination can be released in your organization if action items were this clear: Who's going to do what by when.

Bruce: The power of being clear about priorities and action plans can be seen in this example. I was working with a business implementing this system and I asked one of the associates if they had seen any difference from their efforts in this area. She said, "I have worked for this company and on this team for over 10 years, and I have never seen us accomplish as much as we have this past year. The constant attention to priorities and actions has made a huge difference."

Action plans have an additional benefit. They can help you provide the right amount of oversight over any project. Often as managers we're tempted to go to an extreme: either micromanaging our people or abandoning them. A balance is needed somewhere in the middle, a place where empowerment is found.

An action plan is an effective tool to develop trust *and* accountability. It's easy to review the actions on a regular basis and ask how it's going. The person responsible for implementing the action plan can then show how they're making progress. Not too much control, but not abandonment either.

More Involvement, More Commitment

Once you get clear about these elements—vision, mission, values, objectives, strategies, priorities, and action items—getting things done is easier. Life at work becomes simpler.

After facilitating this process at the most senior level, it's easy to facilitate this process at the next level in the organization.

> *Where all think alike, no one thinks very much.*
>
> –*WALTER LIPPMAN*

When introducing *Prioritize!* to the next level of management, we have found it to be very valuable to have them go through the same planning steps as senior management. People believe in, commit to, and act on what they figure out for themselves. Furthermore, the quality of the plan improves with their input.

It usually takes less time to do this at the management level than at the executive level. As the next layer of management creates their own plan, share with them the elements of the plan created by the senior leaders. In a spirit of win-win, merge the plans with the best elements of each. The result is a plan that the managers buy into.

> *Any enterprise is built by wise planning, becomes strong through common sense, and profits wonderfully by keeping abreast of the facts.*
>
> – *KING SOLOMON*

You may also find it helpful to have the managers repeat elements of this process focused on a smaller segment of the company like a division or department. The vision, mission, values, and objectives would remain the same for everyone, while strategies could be defined at the departmental level. These department strategies link to the company strategies. From there, priorities are still assigned to individuals.

At the end of this process what do you have?

- A strategic plan that can fit on one page
- Top priorities clear for every individual
- Measurements that mark progress
- A feedback system for tracking progress

It's just that simple, that effective, and that cool.

PART 3

The Second Practice: EXECUTE

Communicate

The first step in Execute is communication.

People have to know what the plan is, so you need to tell them.

> *I'll pay more for a man's ability to express himself than for any other quality he might possess.*
>
> – *CHARLES SCHWAB*

Here's one powerful thing we've learned about communication: Get the front line supervisors on board. If they are on board, your communications are going to be fine. If they're not, you may face trouble all through the project.

Bruce: Once I was team leader for a sales team, and I flew in to the company headquarters for our regular monthly meeting. As I checked into my hotel, there was a message that I should join the other team leaders in a meeting with the president of the company the next morning at 7:00 a.m. My boss, Wendy, called me that night to confirm the meeting, but she didn't give me any hints about what was going to happen except that she felt good about it.

The next morning, the 13 sales team leaders and their four regional vice presidents met with the president of the company. The president made a startling announcement: Our company had just signed an agreement to merge with our fiercest competitor!

Stunned, I immediately turned around looking for Wendy sitting a couple of rows behind me. She looked at me, smiled, and gave me a big thumbs up. "So," I exhaled as I thought to myself, "If Wendy thinks this is o.k., then it's probably o.k."

The president went on to give us a detailed explanation as to why this was a forward step for the company and allowed us to ask questions. By the end of the session, I was on board with the merger.

The president made one last appeal. "Our goal today is to get this out in the open, allow some time for people to process it, and then get everyone focused on doing the work that needs to be done today, " he outlined. "What we don't want is a lot of hallway talk and chit-chat about this and taking the focus off our business. You, as team leaders, will have the biggest impact on this. If you can support the change, and keep people focused, it will carry a lot more impact than anything that I, as president, can say."

If people in business told the truth, 80 to 90 percent of their problems would disappear.

– DR. WILLIAM SCHULTZ

At 8:00 a.m. there was a large company-wide meeting to announce this merger. I filed into the large meeting room with about 500 other people. My team members immediately sought me out and started drilling me with questions about the purpose of the meeting. I merely replied, "I can't give you the details, but I think this is a positive step forward."

When the chairman of the board made the same announcement to the assembled audience, there was an audible gasp. The two team members sitting on either side of me leaned over and asked, "Bruce, what do you think of this?" I smiled and gave them a thumbs up. I could see both of them give a big sigh of relief. It was almost as if I could hear them thinking, "If Bruce thinks this is o.k., then it's probably o.k."

And in fact, the day proceeded pretty much like we wanted with everyone focused on getting business done and not on the merger.

What can we learn from this?

The most powerful communicator is the immediate boss, so spend your communication efforts there. What was my first reaction to the news? I looked for Wendy's response. What was the first reaction of my team to the news? They wanted reassurance from me. The president of the company understood this, and that's why he made a direct appeal for our support.

> *What do we live for, if not to make life less difficult for each other?*
>
> – *GEORGE ELIOT*

If someone really wants to know what's going on in your leadership team, would they ask you as one of the leaders, or would they ask the executive assistant who's taking the notes? In almost every case, we tend to trust the person we're closest to, and that often means the person farthest in rank from the president.

For the people in your company, that often means their immediate boss. To get the most buy-in—the best results from your communication efforts—focus there. This is the place where the 80/20 rule applies. Target the supervisors: They're the small group that will get you the biggest and best outcomes.

Four Guidelines for Communicating Direction

Rarely is communication more valuable to an organization than when a leader articulates direction.

Here are a few guidelines:

Make your communication sooner rather than later.

Use your best judgment on this. In the previous example, the vice presidents were informed the evening before. The whole company was in the know by shortly after 8:00 a.m. the next morning. Since one of the strongest signals a person gets regarding their worth to the organization is how soon they're being told about changes, the sooner you can get the word out the better.

> *There are two ways to face the future. One way is with apprehension, the other is with anticipation.*
>
> – *JIM ROHN*

Communicating sooner allows you greater control. By getting the word out quickly, people can be informed by their own leaders. It can be very dispiriting to learn of major news through the grapevine, and the grapevine works very fast. Most people in business hate being surprised, and so they develop strong, effective channels of communication. There are very few secrets.

As a leader, you must repeatedly and consistently communicate your message. It's been suggested that if your people can't give your speech better than you can, you haven't communicated enough. In advertising, it takes at least seven messages to make an impression. Your company is no different. People won't really start believing you until you've said the same thing many times. But don't start counting, just keep repeating.

> *The art of progress is to preserve order amid change and to preserve change amid order.*
>
> *–ALFRED NORTH WHITEHEAD*

Your message serves to bring order out of chaos. Remember, clarify and simplify, clarify and simplify.

Here is one example of how to communicate the results of your strategic planning retreat to those who did not attend. When you get back, call a short meeting with your team.

- Tell them you had fun and you worked hard. You're pleased with the results. (After all, you've gotten to go "play" while they've had to continue grinding out the work. They're anxious to hear how you thought it went.)
- Go through the plan in a systematic way. Start with vision, mission, and values. Show how these are achieved by implementing your strategies and how your progress is measured by your objectives. Finally,

end with your top priorities. Allow time for some questions, and tell how future questions and communications will be handled.

- Make a "by the way" comment. Tell a short story about how your respect has grown for one or more members of the executive team. This will do more for creating trust in the executive team and the plan than any other single thing you can do. This is especially true if the other executive is someone you or your department has not gotten along with in the past.
- End by reinforcing to your team the vital importance of their work (how much you appreciate their talent and their contribution) and why it's so important to get refocused on that work right away.

Greg is a consultant who worked with General Electric during the turn-around years. He said that Jack Welch gave people the same message over and over and over again. He had heard it so often that he was still able to recite it years later. The speech included a brief paraphrase of the current realities, vision, strategic direction and the benefits of change. Some have called it his "elevator speech," a message that could inspire change during an elevator ride. Here it is:

"The *need* is to make GE less bureaucratic. We must free up our employees to focus on customer-valued work. We must get rid of low-value work, activity, reports, meetings, forms, etc.

"Our *vision* is to develop a culture with greater speed, simplicity and self-confidence. We can break down the boundaries and free people to act as entrepreneurs as in small companies.

"Our *strategy* is to empower people closest to the actual work to fix their problems and simplify their process using a 'workout' approach.

"The *benefits* will be streamlined, faster processes, less bureaucracy, and a new culture of empowered people creating greater customer value and profit."

You might consider the benefit of working out your own elevator speech. For many people, they won't really believe you until they've heard you give it many, many times. Don't worry about getting it perfect. Get it as perfect as you can, and when you need to, change it.

Why Don't We Execute our Plans?

In a word, *inertia*.

Let's face it—establishing new habits is difficult.

A habit can have profound impact because it allows us to do something repeatedly without giving it much thought. We don't have to think about how we dress ourselves, how to start the car, or how to write with a pencil.

> *The greatest results in life are usually attained by simple means and the exercise of ordinary qualities. These may for the most part be summed up in these two – common sense and perseverance.*
>
> – OWEN FELTHAM

But that's the problem with creating a new habit—when we're not thinking, we perform the old habits automatically.

The same is true in establishing a high-performance organization. The old habit patterns will emerge when we're not paying attention to what we're doing.

Every company interested in implementing significant change will need to overcome the inertia of old habits.

Establishing a new habit can be like starting a car. When you put the key into the ignition and turn it, the starter puts out a short burst of energy that gets the motor working. Once the motor is running, the starter stops.

In establishing a new habit, the difficulty is often not with the motor, it's with cranking the starter. For example, if I try to start a new regimen of running on a regular basis, I find that the most difficult part is getting my running shoes on. Once I have them on, I almost always go running. It's really not the long run that keeps me from running; it's just getting my shoes on. Putting my shoes on is like the starter in a car; the running takes over automatically, like the motor in the car.

A new corporate habit can be established in the same way. Suppose you get really clear about your top priorities and those of your team. You know it's important to review progress on them regularly (which we'll be discussing in the next section). You can easily establish a new habit by finding your starter—*printing a summary of everyone's priorities for distribution at the meeting*. Once you've handed them out, your motor takes over—it's automatic to review them as a group.

As I grow older, I pay less attention to what men say. I just watch what they do.

–ANDREW CARNEGIE

A very successful bank in the southern United States utilizes this high-performance system. The President worked with us to develop an initial draft of their One Page Strategic Plan. Then, we facilitated strategic planning sessions with his executive team, branch managers, and Board of Directors. Everyone got on the same page and put their Priorities on **www.prioritize.com**.

The next week, they began their regular progress reviews (the starter). The team continues to accomplish extraordinary business results (the motor takes over).

If you want to lead your organization to a higher level of contribution, you need to overcome the inertia of past habits.

Using this starter idea is another example of the 80/20 Principle in action. A little bit of action here leads to big results later. So take the first step. Initiate action. It's often easier than you think.

Priorities are Important But Not Urgent

How do we make all this priority stuff work in the daily grind of business? It's one thing to define the plan in the relative calm of a workshop; it's another thing to execute day-to-day, week-to-week.

Anything less than a conscious commitment to the important is an unconscious commitment to the unimportant.

– Roger Merrill

To help you execute your most important priorities, we'd like to visit a powerful teaching model, popularized by Stephen R. Covey, called the Time Management Matrix.

The Matrix suggests that there are two types of demands on our time: Those things that are important (contributing to our aspirations, strategies and priorities) and those things that are urgent (appearing to require immediate attention). The combinations are displayed in this Matrix:

	Urgent	**Not Urgent**
Important	I: Gets Done	II: Opportunity
Not Important	III: Deception	IV: Waste

The key to effective time management is to habitually do the things that are important!

Things that are important and urgent (Quadrant I) get done or we're looking for a new opportunity in life—we're fired! So, obviously, everything that's important and not getting done is in Quadrant II.

So here is a really big idea: A focus on Quadrant II is *foundational* to creating high-performance.

So what are some Quadrant II activities? Here are a few defining questions:

- Does it serve customers, employees, or owners?
- Does it reflect the 80/20 Principle?
- Does it *prevent* problems, not just *solve* problems?
- Does it build relationships?
- Does it increase capacity?
- Does it develop leaders?

> *For it is the willingness of people to give of themselves over and above the demands of the job that distinguishes the great from the merely adequate organization.*
>
> *–PETER DRUCKER*

Here's the problem, though—Quadrant II priorities are not urgent, so they don't demand our attention. If you're in the swamp with the alligators, it's hard to think about draining the swamp. But if you never take the time to drain the swamp, how will you ever get rid of the alligators? Even a little draining may get rid of a few alligators. That will give you more time to do more draining.

So it is with your time. Any time spent working on your Quadrant II priorities should help prevent time spent in the urgency quadrants. You are therefore freed up to spend more time in building systems or working on the 80/20 items for your customers, employees, and owners while you develop your leaders.

Measurements:
The Foundation for Execution

In the game of business, just like in any other game, you'll have more fun and be more productive if you keep score.

Setting up the right measurements for your company, then, is foundational to execution. How can you tell how you're doing or even if you're making progress, if you're not measuring the right things?

> *Managers without performance measures for their areas of responsibility are like travelers without a way, pilots flying blind, or doctors without a stethoscope – they are working harder and accomplishing less than they otherwise could.*
>
> –WILL KAYDOS

Here are some guidelines about setting up your measurements:

<u>Measure what matters</u>. Some measurements may be common to all businesses and accessing that information may be relatively easy. Your financial statements, for example, can provide you with net profit. Other measurements, like the life-

time value of a customer, may be more difficult. You may not be collecting the information you need, or it may be scattered among several people. Getting the right measurements identified and then tracked may require some trials. Test them out for a while. Typically, you'll find that you need to tweak the way you're calculating your numbers to get them to tell you what you really need to know.

One construction company wanted to know what their labor costs were, but after thinking about it, the managers realized that what they really wanted to know is if their jobs were being profitable. This required measuring each job by labor and parts and then comparing these to the revenue for that job. By measuring labor as a percentage of revenue, they're able to determine quickly if labor costs are reasonable. And they can track this over time by crew, by customer, by job, by department, and by the company as a whole.

The problem in measurement comes from the way it is used. If it is used to punish, people will go to extraordinary lengths to avoid being measured.

– AUBREY C. DANIELS

Good measures balance each other. If you're measuring customer loyalty, you should also measure employee loyalty, since one can be increased at the expense of the other in the short term. If you're measuring net profit, you'll want to measure cash flow, since it's possible to be very profitable and still go out of business if you run out of cash.

Not everything important is measurable and not everything that's measurable is important. Be careful not to measure too much or too little. Some measurements are useful for a while and then they're not. Step back on a regular basis and look at the big picture, then use your wisdom to add or subtract measures from your system.

Don't just ask for information. Many leaders and managers in a company don't invest in building a thorough, dependable measurement system. Instead, they just ask for information randomly from their staffs or accountants. This wastes time and energy and it kills morale. Talk to other leaders in similar businesses to see what they're measuring. Discuss the measures with your accountant and the other leaders in your organization. Then invest your efforts in collecting and displaying the data systematically.

Set up your measurement system. Here are the elements of a dependable measuring system:

- Measuring the right things
- Taking measurements at the right frequency
- Knowing what the minimum, satisfactory, and outstanding levels are
- Graphing the results when appropriate
- Having the right people collect and analyze the information
- Sharing the information with the right people
- Determining what adjustments to make in your systems based on the story that the measurements are telling you

With a good measurement system in place, you can know whether you're succeeding and where you need to focus attention.

Making Progress I: Tracking Results

Once you set up your measurements, it's critical to determine minimum, satisfactory, and outstanding performance for each measure. You must be able to know if the measurements are telling you good news or bad news. If labor is averaging 22%of your installation revenue, is that a good thing or a bad thing? You need to know.

> *How would you like to attend a basketball game where no one kept score, or watch a golf tournament without knowing the players' standings? Not much point, is there? Not much fun either.*
>
> *– JERRY HANEY*

A graph is worth a thousand mental calculations. A graph can tell a story at a glance. See how easy it is to know what's going on when the significant measures of your organization are being displayed like this:

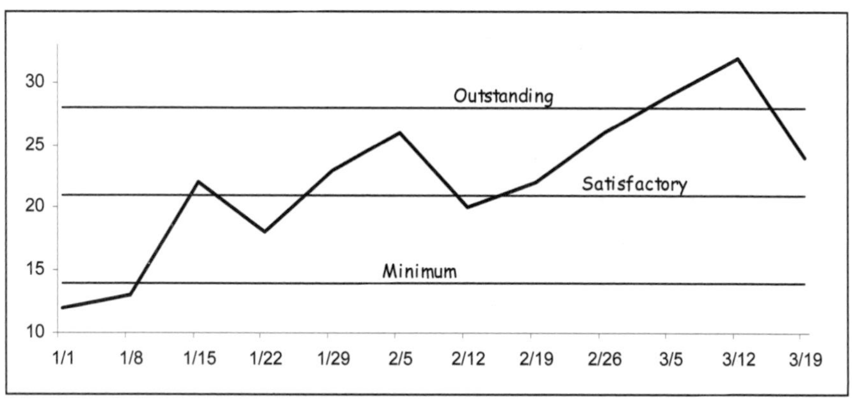

Rather than searching through piles of reports, numbers, tables, and figures, by looking at this graph, you can immediately tell how this particular measure is doing. Compare this graph to a set of numbers that contain the same information:

Time	Production
1/1	12
1/8	13
1/15	22
1/22	18
1/29	23
2/5	26
2/12	20
2/19	22
2/26	26
3/5	29
3/12	32
3/19	24

Minimum: 14
Satisfactory: 21
Outstanding: 28

You can immediately see the value of the graph. Once you get used to seeing graphs demonstrate how your organization is doing on its key performance indicators, you'll be able to quickly grasp how you're doing. Instead of using valuable time trying to figure out what's going on, you'll be able to start making decisions on what to do about it.

> *The real way to enjoy playing golf is to take pleasure not in the score, but in the execution of the strokes.*
>
> – *BOBBY JONES*

Another way to track progress is to use action plans. For example, how would you track the progress of hiring a new person for your accounting work? It wouldn't make sense to graph that particular project, but an action plan would give you an immediate sense of progress:

- ☑ Update job description
- ☑ Review salary
- ☐ Advertise on Internet and in local paper
- ☐ Review resumes
- ☐ Invite top 3 candidates for interviews
- ☐ Make job offer and determine starting date
- ☐ Notify other candidates

Whether you are graphing results or using an action plan, it's easy to grasp the simplicity and clarity of these visual displays.

Making Progress II: Regular Progress Reviews

Teams that execute well communicate often about their progress.

If there's one tool that will help your team execute their priorities, it's the Regular Progress Review. This is the time where delivery, outcomes, and results are monitored and kept on track. *If you want to execute well, you must conduct regular progress reviews. There is no substitute.*

Our friend Barry just lost 54 pounds. He'd wanted to do this for years but had never made any progress. Then he joined Weight Watchers. Guess what aspect of the Weight Watcher program to which he attributes his success? The weekly weigh-ins. There's just something about regular progress reviews that creates extraordinary results.

Once you've identified your top priorities, you'll want to make progress. So, get your team together and create an agenda for a regular meeting where everyone reviews their progress.

We suggest meeting every week or two, though we know companies that meet monthly, and we know companies that meet daily. You'll find the frequency that meets your needs.

How do most team meetings go? The tendency is to conduct a series of one-on-one conversations between the boss and his direct reports. This is a huge waste for the other people in the meeting.

One of our clients has worked to streamline the weekly Progress Review meeting. The leader there makes sure the Reviews are *focused*. Here is their five part agenda that can lead to more effective meetings:

1. Check-in. Each person shares one word that describes their current state of mind. "Tired." "Encouraged." "Pleased." "Frustrated." That's it. No elaboration. It lets everyone know how everyone else is doing. People go in the same order every meeting. It saves time. If someone is missing everyone knows who's next.
2. Clarify Direction. The meeting leader reiterates the aspirations of the organizations—its mission, vision, and values. The purpose of the meeting is described in that context.
3. Share Progress. Using the same order, each person shares their progress on their top priorities. This team uses the stoplight system. "Of my top five priorities, I have two green, two yellow, and one red." (Green means they're on track to make your time frame. Yel-

low means they're close or not sure. Red means they know they're not going to make it.) Then for each light, briefly mention what the status is and the Next Step they're going to take.

4. Summary. The meeting leader or a scribe briefly summarizes the Next Steps coming out of this meeting.
5. Inspirational close. The meeting leader shares an inspiring story or quote to close the meeting on a high note. Stories about people in the company doing outstanding work is often a way he ends the meeting.

Here are some additional guidelines for conducting effective Progress Reviews:

- Shoot for 30-45 minute meetings (less if you're meeting daily, more if you're meeting monthly). Additional conversations should be postponed to a later time. It may be helpful to conduct this meeting as part of another meeting you're already holding.
- Meet on a regular schedule. If everybody can't be there, hold the meeting anyway. People on the road should call in. If you keep the meetings short, people are more motivated to come.
- Avoid digressions or extended problem-solving. Just move it to an after-meeting time slot.
- After the meeting, the only thing that needs to get distributed is the summary of Next Steps. People often need to be reminded of their commitments.

Execution requires regular progress reviews.

Making Progress III: Taking "Next Steps"

One of the most valuable aspects of the Progress Review is to identify Next Steps.

The value of the Next Step is tremendous. Too much time, effort, and frustration come as a result of failure to identify the Next Steps. In other words, work is left standing in the middle of the staircase.

On course doesn't mean perfect. On course means that even when things don't go perfectly, you are still going in the right direction.

– CHARLES GARFIELD

Imagine a business leadership team at their weekly meeting. Here's what you're hearing:

"We really ought to pay attention to that."

"This is becoming a bigger issue."

"I want to see better results on this next month."

"Donna, I want you to look into that."

"Marketing needs to work this out with manufacturing."

Now these comments aren't bad in themselves, but too often, they're the final words on the subject!

A good Next Step helps you make progress rather than just talk about an issue. Here are the elements of a Next Step:

- WHO is going to do
- WHAT by
- WHEN

> *The measure of success is not whether you have a tough problem to deal with, but whether it's the same problem you had last year!*
>
> – *JOHN FOSTER DULLES*

It's just that simple. Until you've identified the WHO, the WHAT, and the WHEN, you don't have a good Next Step.

Here are some examples of Next Steps:

"Jack will talk with purchasing to identify their issues and bring back a recommendation to our next meeting."

"Donna will call the attorney to research options and report back by Tuesday."

"Harry will choose a project team by Friday to analyze the information being passed to manufacturing. They will report their findings by October 15."

Without identifying a WHO, no one takes responsibility. Without a WHAT, it's not clear what should be done. And without a WHEN, it's impossible to prioritize and create accountability.

The key is clarity. If you're not sure what something means, ask.

Bruce: Once I asked a group of customer service reps how long one of their colleagues meant when they said "as soon as possible." The responses seemed to point toward about half a day. Then I asked the group what *they* meant when they said "as soon as possible," and they said they meant a day or two! Same people, two meanings for "as soon as possible!"

A Next Step will avoid that confusion.

It also takes judgment. A good manager will choose a clear WHEN over a certain WHEN. What do we mean by that? Often it's not possible to estimate exactly how long something will take. To hold people strictly accountable for arbitrary dates would not be useful. So it's better to set a clear WHEN and then move it than it is to avoid setting a WHEN. If you don't make it on time, just set another Next Step.

The important thing is to make progress, to keep the work flowing forward. Often, time frames can be adjusted. It's more difficult to restart an effort from a dead standstill.

Developing the habit of identifying Next Steps can be one of the most high-leverage activities performed by you, your team, or your company. It keeps things moving forward, saves time, prevents confusion, avoids false assumptions, and brings accountability to action. A very powerful tool.

Making Progress IV: Persist

Nothing in the world can take the place of persistence. Talent will not; nothing is more common than unsuccessful men with talent. Genius will not; unrewarded genius is almost a proverb. Education will not; the world is full of educated derelicts.

– CALVIN COOLIDGE

We are all called to greatness in some area of life. We're made to dream and achieve, and some of the most important measures of greatness are not what you attain but the magnitude of the obstacles you overcome in the process. Walt Disney failed in business seven times before Mickey Mouse became a household name. Bill Boeing's first aircraft failed. Oprah Winfrey was the first African-American woman to become a billionaire—her teenage parents were Mississippi sharecroppers. Albert Einstein had a learning disability and failed his college entrance exams. 3M began as a failed mining company whose second president could not draw salary for 11 years. *Legends are born in the midst of adversity and persistence.*

There is no failure except in no longer trying.

– ELBERT HUBBARD

It's better to make a small gain and stick with it than to make a huge change and later abandon it. Significant improvements often come more easily when you apply steady, low-level, patient pressure.

Sometime, companies try to surge ahead all at once. Certain events, like a strategic planning day, can help launch a new effort. You can stir up—for a day—a tremendous amount of emotional energy for change. But when you get back to the day-to-day grind, what's really changed three weeks later? Often, not much. It's the persistent, unremitting effort to move forward that's the real test of leadership.

Clarify, Execute, Renew—the three pracitices of *Prioritize!* require unremitting perseverance. There is no substitute.

It can be tough work to change an organizational habit. People will want to avoid accountability. It's hard enough to change a personal habit! And now we're asking to change a *group* habit.

A leader is someone who translates intention into reality and sustains it.

– WARREN BENNIS

But of all the ideas, techniques, and habits that we suggest here in this book, the one that has the longest lasting effect is the Regular Progress Review. The steady, constant movement toward clarifying what's important (Priorities) and the work that has to be done (Next Steps) is what really moves your organization forward.

The message of the Weekly Progress Review is to always clarify, always move forward.

Adjusting Course

If there's one thing we know about strategic planning, it's this: we never get it exactly right.

Things change. Customers' needs change. The economy changes. Technology, employees, our own desires—they all change. You can't just set a course and then head off with blinders on.

The significant problems we face cannot be solved at the same level of thinking we were at when we created them.

–ALBERT EINSTEIN

When a plane flies, being off even one degree can take you miles off course in just a matter of hours. The error can be magnified if you don't adjust for changing winds.

It's the same for a business. Even if we get our planning perfect, if we never make adjustments, we'll still be off course because of the changes in our environment!

Execution is by its nature dynamic. It's like a football game. You do your research, you develop your game plan, you execute the plan, and then, it never works like you thought. Good coaches adjust the game plan as the game goes on. This is one of the basic functions of leadership.

If you and your team play the "game of business" without adjusting, you'll diminish your success. You can only make major directional adjustments when your leadership team steps back to get a fix on where you're going, where you are, and what's going on around you.

> *In the beginner's mind, there are many possibilities; in the expert's mind, there are few.*
>
> *– SHUNYU SUZUKI*

Since you developed your plan with a clear vision, objectives, strategies, and priorities, making adjustments is much easier. Because all work assigned to people is aligned to a strategy, you can clearly see how changing a strategy will affect the work being done. Without this clear line of sight, it will take longer to make all the adjustments necessary. In fact, with clear strategies and priorities, you can make significant course corrections in just a few hours for a large group of people.

There are two ways to make these types of major adjustments to your course: When Needed and Strategic Renewal. The method and the timing are different for each approach.

> *...change is natural and almost always accepted when it produces something positive for the performer.*
>
> *– AUBREY C. DANIELS*

<u>When Needed</u>. Suppose you have a major market event: a competitor steps into (or out of) your marketplace, or new

technology is available, or you gain (or lose) a significant player in your company. You will need to adjust your direction immediately.

Assemble your group of leaders and explain how your situation has changed. This may require some expert input. Discuss in detail how the change may affect your business in all its aspects: marketing, sales, customer retention, employee retention, operations, administration, production.

Next, examine how these changes will impact your strategies. There may be threats you have to defend yourself against or opportunities you can now take advantage of. Make the appropriate changes.

Then identify what priorities need to be established to implement your new strategies. Assign those priorities to the right people.

Once you have new priorities assigned (and some old ones delayed or discarded), you go back to execution: Weekly Reviews and Next Steps.

Adjusting course is made easier when you have your plan in place. As you make adjustments over time, you and your entire leadership team will make them faster, quicker, and more accurately. You will get better at this process, and your people will develop pride at how nimble they can be as they work together.

The second approach to making adjustments, Strategic Renewal, is covered in the next section.

PART

4

The Third Practice: RENEW

Leadership and Organizational Renewal

In 1903, after two failed start-ups, Henry Ford founded the Ford Motor Company. He was almost 40 years old. A few years later, Henry declared his Vision and Mission, "[To] build a motor car for the great multitude…It will be so low in price that no man making a good salary will be unable to own one—and enjoy with his family the blessing of hours of pleasure in God's great open spaces…everyone will be able to afford one, and everyone will have one. The horse will have disappeared from our highways; the automobile will be taken for granted."

> *Inside every old company is a new company waiting to be born.*
>
> *—ALVIN TOFFLER*

In 1908, large numbers of customers were buying Model Ts for $825 each, employees were earning a couple dollars a day (not an unreasonable wage for that time), and the company earned $3 million in net profit.

By 1913, the assembly-line had created tremendous efficiencies, but was burning out employees. The company hired 10 employees to retain one. (And you thought *you* had turnover problems.) Obviously, the company needed to make some adjustments. Henry's answer was announced on January 5, 1914. He would pay people $5 a day plus benefits. Many people thought he was crazy or worse.

But the adjustments produced dramatic results. At the end of 1914, the price of the Model T had been cut in half. Market share increased by 500%, and profits were up by 800%. Even the employees could buy a Ford. Henry's Vision and Mission were being fulfilled.

By 1927, more major adjustments were necessary. Fifteen million Americans had purchased the Model T but the marketplace was again demanding change. People wanted style, not just utility, and GM's Chevrolet had become a formidable competitor. Because Ford was slow to adapt, he was forced to lay off virtually the entire workforce for six months while they prepared to release the Model A. After the triumphal unveiling, Ford reclaimed his leadership position in the industry.

Learning is not compulsory – neither is survival.

– W. EDWARDS DEMING

But, as they say, "Success breeds failure," and in the early 1980's Ford was once again slow to adapt to a rapidly changing marketplace. Customer demand for smaller, fuel-efficient cars had caused Ford to lose $3.3 billion (43% of its net worth) in just three years.

As told in *Built to Last,* the company paused and returned to its long-term philosophy (*aspirations*) articulated by Henry Ford, *67 years earlier.* "I don't believe we should make such an awful profit on our cars. A reasonable profit is right, but not too much. I hold that it is better to sell a large number of cars at a reasonably small profit...I hold this because it enables a larger number of people to buy and enjoy the use of a car and because it gives a larger number of men employment at good wages. Those are the two aims I have in life."

During this process Ford executives re-created their Mission, Values, and Guiding Principles. Former Ford CEO Don Petersen said, "There was a great deal of talk about the sequence of the three P's—people, products, and profits. It was decided that people should absolutely come first [products second and profits third]."

We generally change ourselves for one of these two reasons: inspiration or desperation.

–JIM ROHN

Ford mobilized its people and a $3.25 billion budget to develop a new product—the Taurus/Sable. They solicited input from production workers and customers, monitored dealer service, and in hundreds of ways translated their Vision into daily practice.

The turn-around was remarkable. Taurus/Sable sold more cars than the Model T.

Even when there are no significant events going on in your marketplace, you will want to make adjustments to your plan and its execution. You don't have to experience employee pain, customer pain, or financial pain to make minor adjustments in your ever-changing environment.

To facilitate this process, our system calls for quarterly renewals.

There are two types of Renewals:

- Leadership Renewals are strategic in nature (The Plan)
- Organizational Renewals are inspirational and educational in nature (The People)

The Leadership Renewal paves the way for the Organizational Renewal. Both can follow a similar format, though the individual activities may be different.

We want to be a company that is constantly renewing itself, shedding the past, adapting to change.

– JACK WELCH

Here's an outline for an effective and thorough renewal. Each element will be discussed in greater detail in the following chapters. Together, these steps form the acronym SPIRIT, forming the third step to our system: Renew the SPIRIT.

Following these steps in order may be very useful for your first few renewals. After that, you may want to customize the items and the order to meet the needs of your group.

Significance. A great way to start a renewal is to acknowledge the contributions of each individual and team.

Passion. It's helpful to reconnect to your long-term aspirations—your larger purpose, the motivation you have for doing this work, and how this work helps to fulfill your larger life calling.

Insights. Learning from experience is good. Learning from the experiences of others is great. You multiply your learning when you learn from others.

Rejuvenation. What are you doing to increase your capacity to contribute? Both individual practices and company initiatives get shared.

Innovation. What parts of your plan need to be adjusted? How can you apply what our insights to going forward?

Top 5 Priorities. Since priorities are mostly written for 90 day time frames, you'll need to create new priorities for the new quarter.

Let's look at each one of these elements in more detail.

SPIRIT: Significance

A powerful way to begin a Renewal session is to acknowledge your people and their contributions.

In larger organizations, people are introduced, departments are recognized, and people are affirmed.

With a smaller group of people the approach can be more personal and powerful. Ron Willingham, a brilliant author of training programs, taught us the "compliment card" technique about 20 years ago:

> *The power of a compliment card is what a person has to think and feel to write it, and what another person has to think and feel to receive it.*
>
> *– RON WILLINGHAM*

Pass out 3x5 cards to each person. Everyone writes the name of the other individuals on the top of the card, one name per card. Then have them write down one or two things they appreciate about that person on the card. Comments must be genuine.

The next step is to set the ground rules for how these are going to be shared. You pick one person to be the Receiver and everybody reads their card about that person, one at a time. After reading the card, the reader hands the card to the Receiver.

It's not always easy to receive acknowledgement and praise. For some of us, it's one of the hardest things we do. Our tendency is to want to push the recognition away, to discount it. We say things like, "I was just doing my job," or "it wasn't really all that hard," or "You know, really it's my team that deserves the credit for that."

We want to prevent this discounting. So, the ground rule is, when you're the Receiver, all you can say is, "Thank you." That's it. You just have to sit there and take it.

Do not let any unwholesome talk come out of your mouths, but only what is helpful for building others up according to their needs, that it may benefit those who listen.

– SAINT PAUL

Another ground rule: Only good things can be shared. You may need to coach your team on this a bit. Items that include implied insults or criticisms such as, "You're not as big a jerk as you used to be," are not allowed.

One more. This exercise is most powerful when you avoid it becoming a big laughing session. Sometimes laughter can be too easily interpreted by the Receiver that the feedback is not sincere. The Receiver would probably never say this, even though most of us might feel this way.

One person at a time is the Receiver. Take your time. Don't rush. Let it soak in.

Months later, you may be surprised that people will still remember this activity more than anything else you did that day.

Larger companies can use the same exercise by breaking people into small groups.

Someone once said, "In business, the only thing worse than failure is success without recognition."

SPIRIT: Passion

There is an old story about a wanderer walking into a small village. He approaches three brick layers. Coming up to the first brick layer, he asks, "What are you doing?"

The first brick layer responds, "Are you daft? I'm laying bricks." He continues muttering to himself as the wanderer approaches the second brick layer.

"What are you doing?" he asks.

"Good morning! I'm building a wall," the second brick layer responds as he goes quietly about his business.

The wanderer approaches the third brick layer and notices that this one is humming to himself.

"What are you doing?" the wanderer asks.

"Thank you for asking!" There's a twinkle in the eye of the third bricklayer. "I'm helping to build a cathedral!"

Which of the brick layers are we? Are we the first bricklayer, letting our mundane, repetitive tasks wear us down untill we think our job is just grinding out an existence, just laying bricks?

Or are we the second brick layer, who sees a little bigger picture but is still primarily focused on his own work? At least this bricklayer wasn't muttering!

Or are we the third brick layer, whose motivation and purpose were inspired about the larger outcome of his work? He could see how his contribution, though small, was making a big difference in the world.

All great things are done for their own sake.

– ROBERT FROST

The second step of the renewal process, Passion, is to help us get the perspective of the third brick layer. This step helps us to reconnect to our deepest motivations, our purpose in life.

People work for many reasons. Some work to collect a paycheck. Some work to express their talents, skills, and abilities. And others work to fulfill a deep inner drive to make their unique contribution to the world. There may be combinations of these, as well as other motivations.

A rock pile ceases to be a rock pile the moment a single man contemplates it, bearing within him the image of a cathedral.

– ANTOINE de SAINT-EXUPERY

Passion is about showing bricklayers that they are building a cathedral, seeking out the higher purpose in whatever it is they're doing. If you look hard enough, you can always find it. Work can be a channel for using our talents and a way to make our unique contribution. It provides another profound benefit: it supports families and it allows people a means to contribute effectively in other parts of their lives like community service or non-profit work.

At the Leadership Renewal, you may have each individual share with the group how work and life has intersected and why that's important to them.

> *Far and away the best prize that life offers is the chance to work hard at work worth doing.*
>
> –*THEODORE ROOSEVELT*

At the Organizational Renewal, it's beneficial to have the leadership review the long-term aspirations of the organization and then tell the stories of how your people are bringing that mission and purpose to life. Share the stories where those contributions are made at work and where those contributions benefit the community.

Passion is about the heart, and stories speak to the heart. So tell the stories.

SPIRIT: Insights

The first "I" in SPIRIT is for Insights. This is the time to capture and internalize what we've been learning.

A Renewal becomes an opportunity to develop your associates. How important is this component of the SPIRIT agenda? A poll conducted by Lewis Harris and Associates on the 1999 Emerging Workforce Study shows that among employees who say their company offers *poor* training opportunities, 41% plan to leave within a year, vs. only 12% of those who rate opportunities *excellent*. High turnover isn't cheap. The survey puts the cost of losing a typical worker at $50,000. So a 1,000-worker company with poor training could lose $14.5 million in turnover alone.

The question isn't: 'What if we train people and they leave?' The question should be: 'What if we don't train people and they stay?'

– BRIAN TRACY

There's so much learning going on in an organization and we often miss it. What one person learns can be immensely useful to someone else, if only there was a way to share it!

Two types of deliberations are helpful here. We call them Lessons and Questions.

A group's wisdom and intelligence are accelerated when people share what they've been learning about their work—how to be more effective or efficient. These are "Lessons."

> *Over the long run, superior performance depends on superior learning.*
>
> *—PETER SENGE*

Second, shared Insights can help a leadership team to identify emerging issues—questions that are arising from their complex marketplace. These are "Questions."

Whether at a Leadership Renewal or an Organizational Renewal, you can share Insights in the same way. Break your group up into small teams, three to four people each. Have them make two lists: "Here's what we've been learning," (your list of Lessons) and "Here's what we're not clear about yet" (your list of Questions).

> *The ability to learn faster than your competition may be the only sustainable competitive advantage.*
>
> *—ARIE DeGEUS*

Give the teams about 10-15 minutes to create their lists. If you have flipcharts available, have each team write their lists on the flipcharts. Then have each team brief the larger group on their Lessons and Questions. Avoid giving people the platform to critique another group's work. This is not a contest, it's about sharing.

Share the Lessons and share the Questions.

SPIRIT: Rejuvenation

Rejuvenate means to "make young again." It's the practice of refreshing and re-energizing.

There are three levels: personal, team, and organizational.

The richest soil, if uncultivated, produces the rankest weeds.
– PLUTARCH

At the personal level, the question is, How Do I Take Care of Me? How do I take care of myself mentally (how I keep myself sharp), physically (how I keep myself fit), and spiritually (how I keep myself motivated and inspired)?

At the interpersonal level, the question is, How Do We Take Care of Us? Here we look at communication (how we keep each other in the know), support (how we support each other with encouragement), and conflict resolution (how we handle issues between us).

At the organizational level, the question is, How Do Our Systems Renew Us? Three leadership tools come to mind: recognition (how we acknowledge good work), rewards (how we reward good work through non-monetary means), and compensation (how business success affects my personal income).

At the Leadership Renewal or the Organizational Renewal, you can identify best practices and share them with the group.

> *To keep a lamp burning we have to keep putting oil in it.*
>
> *–MOTHER TERESA*

One of the most motivating aspects of an Organizational Renewal is when the leadership announces enhancements to compensation and incentives. If there aren't any, leave the whole subject off the agenda and work to put something in place for the next quarterly renewal.

Many of our clients find this to be an outstanding opportunity to provide leadership development at the personal, interpersonal, and organizational levels.

SPIRIT: Innovation

Here's what we've done so far:

- Recognized people's contributions (Significance)
- Reconnected to our passion and purpose (Passion)
- Captured and internalized Lessons and Questions (Insights)
- Shared how we make ourselves, our team, and our company young again (Rejuvenation)

> *To achieve things that you have never achieved before, you must be willing to do things you have never done before.*
>
> – *UNKNOWN*

Now let's start looking ahead.

Innovation is the process of reviewing and updating our company long-term aspirations (mission, vision, values) and objectives and strategies.

In some cases there may be some small adjustments to our aspirations. We may need to clarify our Mission (purpose); our Vision (targeted market, product mix, or scope); or our Values (the guidelines we use for decision making and how we treat each other). Often, there's not a lot of changing that needs to go on here.

In many more cases, we'll need to adjust our objectives and strategies to our current reality. So, given our work in clarifying Insights, what objectives and strategies will best serve us now?

For the leadership team, this can be a very rich and rewarding discussion. We've never worked with a company that got their strategies or objectives quite right the first time. Some major rewriting may need to be done here.

> *If the rate of change inside an organization is slower than the rate of external change – the end is near.*
>
> *– JACK WELCH*

Your goal, at the leadership level, is for a robust dialogue. Encourage a variety of views. Don't try to arrive at a revision too quickly. You've hired a group of great people; why not get the best each has to offer?

New strategies and objectives need to emerge from this dialogue. Then you're ready to take them to the company.

At the company renewal, the level of involvement can vary depending on your situation. Some companies like to have everyone go over the new objectives and strategies and suggest improvements. Some companies want the focus to be on the priorities (which is the next step) so they explain the changes but don't allow for a lot of discussion. How you do it will be up to you.

Innovation paves the way for the next step, Top 5 Priorities. When you're clear about how you're going to reach your vision, Priorities can be more easily written.

SPIRIT: Top Priorities

This is where all the talk becomes action: Top Priorities. Based on everything covered so far, each individual writes their new Top Priorities for the new quarter. Remember the guidelines? Start with a verb, end with a date, have something measurable in between.

> *The key is not to prioritize what's on your schedule, but to schedule your priorities.*
>
> *– STEPHEN R. COVEY*

After you write your Priorities, it's good to have a boss review them, and then it's very helpful to write out Action Plans for implementing them.

Now everyone has a focus for going forward!

The Yearly Pattern of Planning, Execution, and Renewal

Let us draw a picture of an ideal business year. (Remember an ideal is a model, something we strive for. In practice, we need to make adjustments for the reality of the situation.)

Starting point. The first step is the creation of the initial strategic plan. The leadership team clarifies the essential six elements: vision, mission, values, objectives, strategies, and priorities.

> *Much of what we call management simply gets in the way.*
>
> – PETER DRUCKER

Execution. The strategic plan is communicated to others in the organization. Working together, other leaders and managers define their top priorities. Progress reviews are held on a regular schedule (every one or two weeks). Individuals report progress and identify barriers and next steps. Results are measured and tracked.

Renewal. At the end of the quarter the leadership team conducts its first quarterly renewal workshop. The agenda follows the SPIRIT methodology: Significance, Passion, Insights, Rejuvenation, Innovation, Top Priorities.

This pattern of Execution, Renewal, Execution, Renewal, repeats itself until its time for the annual strategic planning workshop, often in the October- January time frame in preparation for the following year.

Here are the tools:

For writing or renewing the strategic plan:

- facilitation techniques for group processes
- methodology to put the plan on a single page

For execution:

- a tool for tracking ongoing progress of priorities
- a Progress Review meeting agenda

For quarterly renewal workshops:

- facilitation techniques for group processes
- the SPIRIT Agenda

It is by the real that we exist, it is by the ideal that we live.

– VICTOR HUGO

This is a system whereby you can keep your entire organization current and on the same page. The amount of time spent in trying to figure out what to do, how to do it, and who should be doing it, is reduced dramatically. Instead, people focus on the work that will serve customers, owners, and employees as you develop leaders on all levels.

The Yearly Pattern of [1]Clarify, [2]Execute, & [3]Renew

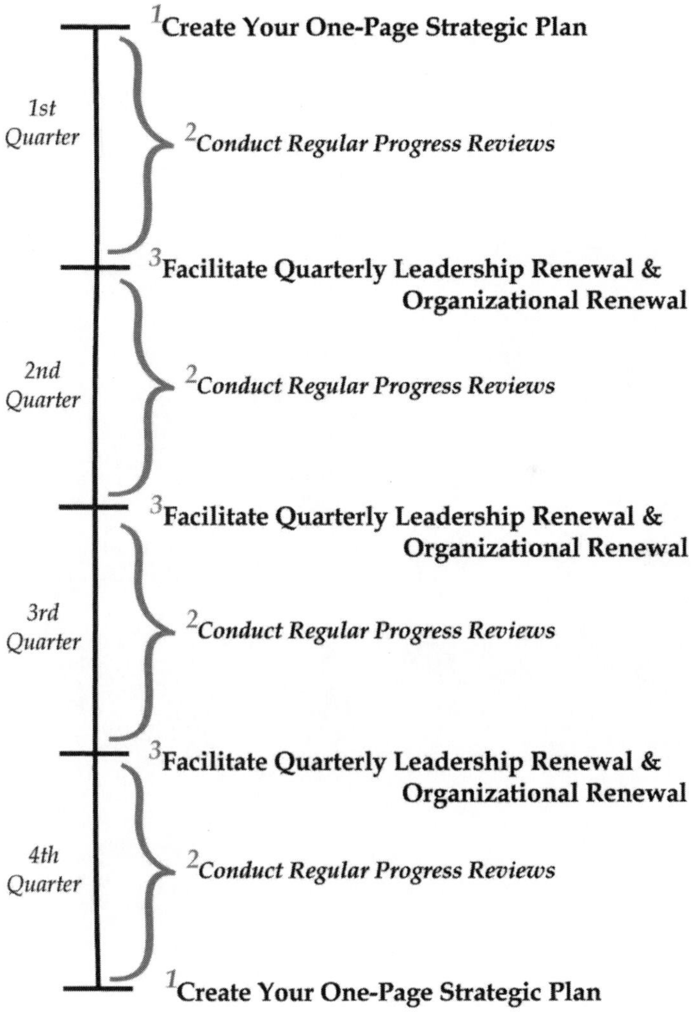

PART 5

APPLY

Putting *Prioritize!* to Work

Let's explore how this leadership system could work for you. What follows is an example of a typical implementation. You may not need to take every step. Every company is unique. No one size fits all, but there are some basic steps that will help you achieve higher levels of performance.

Bobtronics is a small manufacturing firm that makes bobolators, a small electro-mechanical device used in the health care industry. The CEO is Darla Pennington, and she has an executive team of five senior leaders.

The First Practice: Clarify

Darla and her team heard about the *Prioritize!* system from a trusted colleague. She invested in several copies of *Prioritize!* to share with her senior team.

The approach made sense, so Darla and her team decided to schedule a strategic planning workshop. As they completed the pre-work for the workshop, they each made notes about what they felt their vision, mission, values, objectives, strategies, and priorities ought to be. They also jotted down some thoughts on the company's strengths, weaknesses, opportunities, and threats.

During the strategic planning workshop, the senior team achieved consensus regarding their **vision**, **mission**, and **values**. The results were clear, simple statements that described where they wanted to go (vision), their purpose (mission), and how they would govern themselves along the way (values).

In light of their aspirations, the team contemplated their growth in measurable terms. They developed **objectives** and key measures to track their progress. They wanted to keep things simple, so their objectives were about revenue growth, net margin, customer loyalty and team member engagement.

They completed a **S.W.O.T.** analysis, and after brainstorming their strengths, weaknesses, opportunities, and threats, they used multi-voting to prioritize. The exercises kept everyone involved and the best ideas came forward.

Then they created **strategies**. The group identified their strategic categories—the major areas to help them organize their work. They decided on marketing, operations, product development, financial performance, and human resources. Then they wrote specific strategies. For example, here is their human resources strategy: "Release our people's innovation through training and incentives."

They discovered that with well-written strategies, the writing of **priorities** was simple and straightforward. Each member of the leadership team created a Top Priorities list and they shared their priorities with the entire team. Some suggestions were made to improve priorities. They discussed and negotiated time lines and resources. In the end, each person endorsed the priorities of the others.

At the end of the day there was a quiet satisfaction and confidence in having accomplished so much in such a short time. The team now had a plan to implement. What's more, all the senior leaders were on the same page.

Each individual on the team had a stronger desire than ever to accomplish their clear and simple plan. They subscribed to the *Prioritize!* Online Performance System, a system designed to track progress on priorities. Darla gave her team a couple of days to enter their priorities into the Performance System. Two weeks later, they held their first Progress Review meeting.

The Second Practice: Execute Priorities

At their first Progress Review meeting, Darla asked everyone to check in with one word on how they were feeling at that moment. She briefly reviewed their company vision, mission, and values and explained the purpose of the meeting and how it would help them move in the direction of their vision.

Darla then passed out copies of her Team Page from the *Prioritize!* Online Performance System website so that everyone could view the priorities of the entire team.

Her marketing director went first and gave a three minute update on his priorities—which ones were on track, which ones were not. For those that weren't on track, the group helped him clarify his next steps. With only five priorities, there was time for a couple of quick questions. When further discussion was needed, Darla easily directed it to another time outside the meeting.

As each person gave their update, Darla recorded next steps on a notepad. At the end of the meeting, Darla reviewed the next steps as a reminder to everyone what they were committing to do.

She then concluded the meeting with a story about how one of their employees went the extra mile in delivering a package to a client. Darla asked the team to forward her other stories of people who were going the extra mile.

Two weeks later, in their second review, Darla extended the meeting for a few minutes to explore what her team was learning about implementing the *Prioritize!* system. One lesson Darla's team learned was that it's easy to be overly optimistic about how much you can actually get done. There were many distractions, interruptions, and emergencies that competed for time and attention.

Still, her team felt like they were making progress. While not doing everything they'd hoped for, they were accomplishing more than ever before.

After a few weeks, Darla's team decided expand the *Prioritize!* system to the next level of company managers. Darla facilitated a workshop with the managers to refine the company's Vision, Mission, Values, and Objectives, working from the senior team's initial plan. After reviewing the senior team's version, this group decided to suggest some changes.

Then these managers wrote their priorities. As a Next Step, Darla directed each person to review their priorities with their boss by the end of the next week.

As the next couple of weeks passed, Darla and her senior leaders started to notice that the next layer of managers were getting more Quadrant II activities accomplished, and it was clear to everyone that the clarity and simplicity brought greater motivation.

When faced with changes, Darla found that having everyone's priorities clearly outlined was a great help. She could see the big picture at a glance, and then call her leaders together to discuss what priorities need to be changed, adjusted, or delayed so that other more important work could be done.

This was especially true when dealing with a crisis. She called meetings, discussed problems, and assigned new priorities. They reported back within a few hours on how to manage other priorities in light of the changes. Her senior team and their teams were all becoming more nimble in adjusting to changing conditions.

Since the leadership team was getting a bird's eye view of the whole organization on a regular basis, other things started to become clear. As tasks got completed and problems started to get solved, 80/20 thinking started to work at higher levels. Now the senior team started thinking about how to leverage client relationships and special proprietary knowledge for creating new revenue streams. New business ideas were given attention. Departmental life started becoming more balanced, more forward-thinking, and more proactive.

It became clear to the leadership team that there were fewer crises to handle. There were fewer priorities, too, as they applied the 80/20 Principle; priorities tended to be more long-term and higher leverage activities. The whole company started to emerge into a different way of thinking about how it added value to the marketplace.

There was a growing feeling that there were significant opportunities still to come.

The Third Practice: Renew

Darla scheduled the first Quarterly Renewal Workshop about 90 days after the Strategic Planning Workshop. To prepare for the meeting, she sent a survey to all participants and conducted a handful of interviews in preparation. She wanted to know what was working and what wasn't, how much was getting done, and what people were learning.

The leadership team and the next level of managers were all invited to participate in the Renewal Session. There was a spirit of celebration and excitement in the air.

First, Darla spoke about how important it was to acknowledge the team's progress in this renewal setting. A lot had been done and there was much left to do. She pointed out how important it was to step back from everyday work, assess their progress, take stock of lessons learned, and set a new course for going forward.

Following the SPIRIT agenda, she engaged the group in an exercise that affirmed the individuals and their achievements (**Significance**). Some awards were handed out—some serious, some just for fun.

She then guided the group through a series of exercises to help them reconnect to their corporate aspirations (**Passion**), collect the Lessons and Questions (**Insights**), and share ways in which they kept themselves and their teams playing at the top of their game (**Rejuvenate**).

Team members came prepared to talk about going forward. First, they reviewed company strategies. A few of the strategies were adjusted to reflect the current reality (**Innovate**). Then, each individual created a new set of priorities for the new quarter (**Top Priorities**). Some of these priorities moved forward from the last quarter, others were continuations of previous priorities, and still others were new.

Everyone reviewed their new priorities with each other and received feedback. The entire group was getting better at applying the **80/20 Principle**. They were unified behind a fresh, coherent direction—from vision to priorities.

In the months that followed, Darla noticed changes in how her company managed itself. At team meetings, when people committed to actions, someone was always there to write it down and send out action reminders promptly. Rarely did anyone get away with being vague ("I'll get back to you as soon as possible"). Rather, they consistently clarified **Next Steps** in a clear and simple manner.

Cross-departmental rivalry began decreasing dramatically. Fewer people took things personally. There was a sense that corporate priorities needed to take precedence over personal agendas. More issues were being resolved as business issues rather than as personality issues.

As Darla solved more pressing issues, she was able to shift her focus from solving problems to seizing opportunities. The company implemented more training and education about business literacy, markets, product development, and process efficiency. What used to get rewarded—solving crises—was no longer valued as much. More attention was paid to preventing crises, running things smoothly, and being proactive. Darla and her leadership team began to appreciate one another's leadership styles.

Darla's **visionary leadership** style was working in synergy with the **operational leaders** on her team. Setting clear priorities and managing progress provided the right mix for profitable growth. Revenues and net margins were exceeding their objectives. New objectives were established for customer loyalty and team member engagement.

To **simplify and clarify** had become a rhythm of their business. Individuals were getting more done, the company was getting more done, and people were increasing their impact in other areas of their lives.

PART 6

LIVE

Lead a Great Life

While the focus of this book is on building a great business, the context is building a great life. Business can't be your whole life—you'll miss too much.

In our work with thousands of businesses, communities, non-profits, and government leaders over the last couple of decades, we've noticed certain themes keep showing up in the lives of those leaders we admire.

> *The future belongs to those who believe in the beauty of their dreams.*
>
> – *ELEANOR ROOSEVELT*

These are some of the parallels between leading a great life and leading a great organization.

Great Organizations	**Great Leaders**
Clarify Direction	Discover their Calling
Execute Priorities	Make Unique Contributions
Renew the Spirit	Expand their Capacity

Let's look at each of these in more detail.

Discover Your Calling

It takes great courage for men and women to discover their calling. After all, it may not be what you're doing now, and to face your calling squarely may cause some significant disruption in your life.

Somehow, we human beings are never happier than when we are expressing the deepest gifts that are truly us.

– OS GUINESS

One of the most appealing aspects about discovering your calling is its resounding truth. When you discover your calling, it feels like you're being most true to you. It's not about obligation. It's not about duty. It's about following your heart's deepest desire.

It's a discovery about what's already been a part of us from the beginning. Because we've become separated from it, we need to discover it again.

Here are some aspects of a calling that may help you discover yours:

It's yours alone. A calling is unique. It can't belong to anyone else because it calls on your uniqueness. No one else can serve in your place, even if they want to. You are different from anyone else in the world, even if you share the same genetic code with your twin.

> *The man who is born with a talent which he is meant to use, finds his greatest happiness in using it.*
>
> *– JOHANN GOETHE*

It calls on your unique gifts. You can serve in a way and in a place that no one else on earth can. Your calling will demand that of you. Even if you're in a position or hold a title that many others have (e.g., Customer Service Rep), your unique abilities will allow you to perform that job in a way no one else can.

It calls on your unique desires. The magic of a calling is that you don't tire of it. You get to do what gives you joy over and over! (If you don't know what we're talking about, you haven't found it. That's o.k.! Keep searching!)

> *A musician must make music, an artist must paint, a poet must write if he is to be ultimately at peace with himself. What one can be, one must be.*
>
> *– ABRAHAM MASLOW*

Your calling gives you strength and keeps you humble. By recognizing your calling, you gain the grace to acknowledge others in their callings, in their set of unique gifts and abilities. You have no need to appear more important than you already are. On the other hand, you lose the false modesty that says you're not good at anything. You grow in the quiet confidence that you do make a difference and that you're *supposed* to do so.

Discovering your calling can be the result of a moment or the unfolding of years. Each person comes to it on their own path—some at six, others at 60. For many people, their calling will shift as they move into different seasons of life. For a while their calling may be to raise children, then to lead a community service effort, then to start their own business.

O.K., so what do you do when your calling is so far away from what you're doing now? Do you just abandon everything to go after it?

Many persons have the wrong idea about what constitutes true happiness. It is not attained through self-gratification but through fidelity to a worthy purpose.

– HELEN KELLER

In most cases, the answer is *no*. It's not good to walk away from your responsibilities and the people that depend on you, especially if those people happen to be your spouse and your children. Instead of looking at this as an either/or proposition—"Either I can follow my calling or I can uphold my responsibilities, but I can't do it all"—use all your wisdom and the wisdom of others around you to find a way to do both. The better question is, "How can I move closer to my calling while upholding my responsibilities?"

We can do no great things – only small things with great love.

– MOTHER THERESA

Joe: For a time when I worked with Stephen R. Covey, I went to work three quarter time for three quarter pay. I chose to invest one quarter of my time to pursue more significant desires. I used my unique abilities to make broader contributions to the world, my community, and my family. At other times, especially when leading my own business, I've felt called to work 125%.

Over time, you will find opportunities to live out your calling more deeply. And that will bring joy to you and to others near you.

We've seen people fall in love with life when they *begin* to pursue their calling. They may be in the midst of great challenge, but there's a calm that underlies their life because they know they're doing what they're supposed to be doing.

Pay attention to your heart. Begin there. Listen carefully. Then work that into your life like yeast into dough. It will permeate everything, and transform you in the process.

Make Your Unique Contribution

If 'calling' is responding to your heart, then 'contribution' is using your head and your hands to make a difference.

> *We make a living by what we get, we make a life by what we give.*
>
> – WINSTON CHURCHILL

The principle here is *giving*. It's really very simple: the more you give, the more you receive. Many people we've known have reached the point in their lives that giving becomes their primary motivation. The joy, satisfaction, and fulfillment that come from giving are so profound that they want to do it more and more. Or as Etienne de Grellet put it, "I shall pass through this world but once. Any good thing therefore I can do, or any kindness that I can show to any human being, let me do it now. Let me not defer it or ne-

> *You can have everything in life you want if you can help enough other people get what they want.*
>
> – ZIG ZIGLAR

glect it, for I shall not pass this way again."

Your unique contribution is the giving of yourself, your talents, insights, and resources in all areas of your life. It's this giving that blesses others and in turn gives you great joy.

And there's a surprise that awaits most people as they make their unique contribution. It's *easier than they think,* but what's easy for them turns out to be incredibly valuable for others. The fact that it's easy disguises how unique and valuable it can be.

You are the only one who can do your part.

– KRIS KING

There are many things in the world others are good at that we're not good at. Just think of all the talents and abilities in the world: from glass blowing to speaking multiple languages, from playing baseball to caring for the mentally ill, from computing taxes for your business to working a printing press.

And we are good at many things. We each have an incredible array of talents, abilities, and experiences in our repertoires. We can work with people, numbers or ideas; organize action, see possibilities, or design results-driven systems.

The problem with having so many talents and abilities is that they may hide what we're *uniquely* suited for. Something that comes easily to us, that makes a significant contribution, and that gives us joy in doing.

Let us endeavor so to live that when we come to die even the undertaker will be sorry.

– MARK TWAIN

Making your contribution is an ongoing journey and a labor of love. Sometimes the perspective of people we know helps us find the niche where our heads and hands will make the most significant impact.

Dan Sullivan of *The Strategic Coach* suggests you ask ten people who know you well what they think you do that is uniquely valuable. You may be surprised at what you find!

Build Your Capacity

Calling, Contribution, and Capacity are interrelated. They reinforce each other. As you discover your calling and build your capacity, you are able to make greater contributions. Neglecting any of these areas diminishes your potential.

> *The major question to ask on the job is not what you are getting, the major question to ask on the job is what you are becoming.*
>
> *–JIM ROHN*

Capacity relates to size, particularly to your ability to respond to the size of your calling and your contribution. Increasing your capacity comes from developing yourself in several distinctive ways.

Spiritual. This is where we find our inspiration. The root word of "inspiration" is inspire, which relates to breathing in. What fills you up? What breathes life into you? For most of us, our sources of inspiration run deep, and we must not be afraid to make deep demands on them.

Mental. Certainly we can develop our abilities to have more wisdom, insight, understanding and knowledge.

We can develop our mental capacity to see the problem behind the problem and the question behind the question. We can learn to read people better, and to make better decisions. Reading, listening, thinking, meditating, and journaling are all aids in this.

You can change what you are where you are by changing what goes into your mind.

– ZIG ZIGLAR

Relational. Our contribution—and what we receive from it—will bless those we are closest to. Our families, for example, receive the financial benefit from our jobs or our business interests. Life with them is enhanced by your happiness. But it's also true that our jobs and businesses benefit from the contribution our families make to us. So nurturing the close relationships we have increases our ability to make our unique contribution in the marketplace.

What can be added to the happiness of a man who is in health, out of debt, and has a clear conscience?

– ADAM SMITH

Often, our ability to contribute does not rely on our personal capacity but on the size and quality of our network. It's not necessarily what we can do...it's who we know that can help. Our ability to contribute is then multiplied by all the people that we can call upon and ask for help.

Physical. A life of purpose is what the body, mind, and spirit crave; and our life achievements are the fruits we contribute back. By keeping our bodies fit, we expand our ability to contribute. Endurance, strength, flexibility, and coordination become the means by which we can increase our contribution in any area of life. The invisible connection between our bodies, minds and spirits—no longer theory, but fact—must be tended just as any business, garden, or automobile must for peak performance. Attention to it consists of basic actions that make purpose shine—just as with your One Page Strategic Plan.

A life that does not receive exercise, good food and quiet time cannot return vitality. Those elements are your body's "fundamentals." A body starved of them loses the force that helps fuel purpose...and a diminished sense of purpose will cause stress.

A balanced life is essential to our peak performance. By keeping our bodies fit, we expand our ability to contribute; and endurance, strength, flexibility, and coordination become the means by which we can increase that contribution. Do not forget to water the tree that will bear the fruit of contribution. You are that tree!

Financial. Most of us have enough financial capacity to contribute to causes or movements that we think are important. But how much more could we contribute if we were prosperous? How many of us are trapped in jobs or careers or businesses because of financial concerns? So, to be able to contribute more in the way that we're uniquely qualified, we must also develop our financial capacity. We must strive to first be financially intelligent, and then to have financial abundance—enough to provide for others. Abundance is not determined by what you have, but by how receptive you are, how well you steward your resources,

The hardest victory is the victory over self.

–ARISTOTLE

and how fully you share them. We've all known people who apparently have more than enough but keep striving for more, discontented and unsatisfied. They lack abundance. And we know others with modest incomes who reflect an aura of plenty by their generous giving.

Building our capacity, making our unique contribution, being true to our deepest calling—these make our lives whole. And to the extent that we grow in these things, they are certain to have a positive impact on the organizations we lead as well.

Put Your Business Life in Perspective

So, what are the parts that make your life whole? What's your life about?

As you think about the parts of your life, which parts are most important—family relationships, vibrant health, personal faith, meaningful contributions at work, a satisfying hobby, a volunteer role, financial stewardship?

As we explore business success, let's put it into perspective. Take a moment now to identify the most important priorities in your life. Write them on a card and stick it in your wallet or purse!

To keep your life in perspective, consider this: the better your business, the more choices and resources you will have to help you enjoy all the other passions and responsibilities of your life.

Afterword

How Does the World Pass Us By?

Sometimes, when we look back on our business, we wonder where the time has gone. Sometimes we're pleased with what we've been able to accomplish, and sometimes we're not. We wonder how we could have let so much time go by and still not have done some of the things we set out to do.

> *It is an old and ironic habit of human beings to run faster when we have lost our way.*
>
> – *ROLLO MAY*

When things aren't going quite right, the temptation is to struggle with feelings of frustration, guilt, and bitterness. Even when we know it's not healthy for us or those around us to indulge such feelings, what else can we do?

Joe: Several years ago, I learned a valuable lesson about priorities. After an extended international trip, I returned to my office in Kansas City with a serious case of jet lag. And, of course, I returned to a large stack of items that required my attention. I was so tired, that without thinking, I began addressing the items one at a time from the top of the stack.

You've probably heard of the "ABC" prioritizing technique. Rate an item's importance with an "A," "B," or "C." "A" means that I need to do it today, "B" that I'd like to do it today, and "C" means that it's not necessary to get it done today. They you number the priorities in order of importance—do A1 first, then A2, then A3, etc. Well, knowing and doing are two different things.

So imagine that stack, and remember I was addressing the items one at a time from the top. Based on their real priority, it went something like this: B4, A5, C10, B14, A7, C3. It wasn't until a little before 5:00 p.m. that I got to my A2 priority. A little *after* 5:00 p.m. I finally found my A1 priority. But it was too late. The day was over. What a valuable lesson!

And this is the way it goes too often. Without thinking through our priorities, individuals and organizations waste an incredible amount of time and under-serve their customers, team members, and owners. The day, the week, the quarter, the year, *the life* end with A1 still to accomplish.

> *Once you recognize that the…primary purpose of your business is to serve your life, you can then go to work* on *your business, rather than* in *it.*
>
> —MICHAEL E. GERBER

Here's the point. If we spend our time working *in* the business or *in* our lives, instead of working *on* our business or *on* our lives, it's like running through the same old stack in our in-basket. But when we focus *on* our business and *on* our life, we accomplish what's most important.

Note the key here is first to *notice what's going* on and then, *do something about it*. It's when we're paying attention that life doesn't seem to just pass us by. We're involved, we're conscious, we're awake, and we're participating.

Great minds have purposes, others have wishes.
– WASHINGTON IRVING

It's helped us to see ourselves as part of a big, big story. Our purpose is crucial to the outcome, and we have many obstacles to face, just like the heroes and heroines face in the great stories and movies that speak so strongly to our hearts. Once we see the big story, then life doesn't seem to pass by without us knowing it. We live on purpose because we have a significant part to play.

So what's the bigger story for you? And what priorities will shape it?

About The Authors

Joe Calhoon is recognized as one of the nation's leading authorities on leadership development and organizational performance. In the past 20 years, he has given over 2,000 presentations to more than 400 different organizations on four continents. In addition to helping start more than 20 new businesses, Joe has been recognized as National Management Coordinator of the Year, and an Outstanding Young Man in America. As a consultant, Joe has helped his clients increase revenues and profits by as much as 400 percent in one year.

Joe is as comfortable keynoting for a group of 1,000 as he is facilitating for a group of senior executives. In 1992, Joe earned the prestigious Certified Speaking Professional (CSP) designation from the National Speakers Association. Fewer than 400 people worldwide hold this designation.

Joe lives in Kansas City, Missouri with his wife, Diane, and their son, Joseph.

Bruce Jeffrey is a leading authority on developing personal success and high-performance leadership teams. For the past 20 years, Bruce has served to increase organizational performance by training, managing, leading, and consulting with Fortune 500 companies, mid-size companies, business start-ups, government, and non-profit organizations.

Bruce has also served as an Air Force officer. His tours of duty include flying on a combat crew and serving on the faculty of the Air Force Academy.

Some of Bruce's clients have included Sprint, Citicorp, Motorola, Ford Motor Company, Kimberly-Clark, Bank of America, DST Systems, Informix, InterContinental Hotels and Resorts, Host Marriott, and General Electric.

Bruce and his wife, Bobbie, live in Kansas City.

Taking the Next Steps

Would you like some help with the specific needs of your business? Joe, Bruce, and their team have extensive experience helping people and businesses achieve higher levels of performance.

Your Name: ______________________________

Company: ______________________________

Address: ______________________________

City, State, Zip: ______________________________

Phone: ______________________________

Email: ______________________________

Please check the products or services you'd like to learn more about:

- ☐ Keynote Speeches or Seminars
- ☐ Leadership Development
- ☐ Strategic Planning
- ☐ Business Evaluation and Consultation
- ☐ The PriorityAdvantage™ Learning System
- ☐ The Prioritize! Online Performance System
- ☐ Other ______________________________

How would you like us to contact you?

- ☐ Phone Call
- ☐ Postal Mail
- ☐ Email
- ☐ Add me to your e-newsletter
  (email address:______________________________)

How to contact us:

- Visit our website: www.prioritize.com
- Call us: 1-816-746-8696
- Fax this page to us: 1-816-746-8695
- Email us: info@prioritize.com

PriorityAdvantage Learning System

You've read Joe and Bruce's book on organizational and personal success, now listen to these business performance authorities on CD!

This powerful, content-rich educational tool (Promotional DVD, 5 Audio CD's, and companion Resource Manual) will show you how to implement the Three Practices in your business and how to focus your entire organization on achieving its highest priorities.

Listen to Joe and Bruce explain the *Prioritize!* system in a conversational format. This is not the book on tape but an audio overview of the system described in this book.

Especially helpful:

- If you like to listen while you drive
- You'd rather hear the message than read it
- You want to deepen your understanding of these principles and practices
- You want your whole team to learn together

Great for drive time and for reviewing during team meetings.

Order now by calling **1-816-746-8696** or by visiting online at **www.prioritize.com**!

Prioritize! Online Performance System

The *Prioritize!* Online Performance System is designed to help you and your company develop leaders as you more effectively meet the needs of customers, employees, and owners.

11 Reasons to Use *Prioritize!* Online Performance System

1. **Performance improves**. Every user focuses on their most important priorities.
2. **Communication increases**. Every user can view the priorities of every other user in their company.
3. **Accountability is made easy**. Every user can see the progress being made by every other user.
4. **Meetings are shorter**. What used to waste hours in meetings can now be viewed in minutes on the web.
5. **People are more connected**. Each user can quickly view the company's big picture as well as progress made by an individual or a team.

6. **Strategic execution is streamlined**. Any user can view on one webpage the progress on all priorities related to a company strategy.
7. **Work becomes more meaningful**. Every person has a direct line-of-sight from their work to company strategies.
8. **Teamwork is enhanced**. Users can view a whole team's progress at a glance. Team members can see who needs help in accomplishing their priorities.
9. **Problem areas are quickly identified**. The Green-Yellow-Red light system allows you to focus on trouble spots quickly.
10. **Your business can quickly adapt to it's changing marketplace**. Users can quickly adjust their priorities to reflect changes in company strategy.
11. **It's easy to use.** Most users can be up and running in less than 15 minutes.

Call 1-816-746-8696 or email us at pops@prioritize.com to subscribe now!